Plato and education

Plato and education

Robin Barrow
School of Education
University of Leicester

Routledge & Kegan Paul
London, Henley and Boston

First published in 1976
by Routledge & Kegan Paul Ltd
39 Store Street,
London WC1E 2DD
Broadway House,
Newtown Road,
Henley-on-Thames
Oxon RG9 1EN and
9 Park Street,
Boston, Mass. 02108, USA
Manuscript typed by Alice Rockwell
Printed in Great Britain
by Redwood Burn Limited
Trowbridge and Esher

ISBN 0 7100 8343 2

The Students Library of Education has been designed to meet the needs of students of Education at Colleges of Education and at University Institutes and Departments. It will also be valuable for practising teachers and educationists. The series takes full account of the latest developments in teacher-training and of new methods and approaches in education. Separate volumes will provide authoritative and up-to-date accounts of the topics within the major fields of sociology, philosophy and history of education, educational psychology, and method. Care has been taken that specialist topics are treated lucidly and usefully for the non-specialist reader. Altogether, the Students Library of Education will provide a comprehensive introduction and guide to anyone concerned with the study of education, and with educational theory and practice.

This book is a sequel to Dr Barrow's highly controversial 'Plato, Utilitarianism and Education' in the International Library of Philosophy of Education. It has, however, a different intention and is written for a rather different type of reader. In his first book Dr Barrow presupposed some views about Plato on the part of his reader and was concerned to defend Plato against his liberal-democratic critics such as Bertrand Russell and Karl Popper. His treatment of Plato was dominated very much by his general thesis that Plato was concerned, above all things, with human happiness.

'Plato and Education', however, is a more elementary exposition of Plato's thought which presupposes no previous acquaintance with it on the part of readers. It concentrates very much on Plato's educational ideas, e.g. about the distribution of education, learning by discovery, the curriculum and intellectual development, art, and moral education. Dr Barrow claims that Plato's greatness lay in his astonishing ability to raise fundamental questions, which are highly relevant today, and to argue a case rationally, penetratingly, and powerfully – a case which is not fashionable today but which has to be met.

Plato was the first philosopher of education and Dr Barrow claims that, in spite of his Utopianism, and his pioneering work in psychology and sociology, the difference between what he was doing and what is done by modern philosophers of education can be exaggerated. Thus his work provides a brilliant introduction to the philosophy of education though, as Dr Barrow admits, 'It is quite likely that much of what Plato has to say will strike modern readers as thoroughly obnoxious – there are many aspects of his point of view which happen to rest ill alongside the current liberal orthodoxy. But he who shares with Plato a passion for the truth, rather than a mean-spirited devotion to his present opinions, will know that the challenge must be seriously examined . . .'

Dr Barrow's book provides an excellent starting point for such an examination as well as an exciting point of entry into most of the major issues in philosophy of education. Most modern philosophers of education, perhaps because of their embarrassment about the not too distant past of their subject, have tended to ignore its history. Dr Barrow's introduction to the subject, via one of the greatest figures in its history, is much to be welcomed.

R. S. PETERS

To Paul Croll, whose critical eye and ingrained suspicion of Plato have helped me, I hope, to be a little more objective than I might otherwise have been.

Contents

Contents

Plato and education

Chapter one

Introduction

WHY PLATO?

In a world that seems increasingly beset by the demand
for instant gratification, by rapid change and by
intense palaeophobia, the first question that has to be
answered is 'Why Plato?' Why write yet another book
about a man, dead for over two thousand years, who belongs
to another age and another civilisation? What can Plato,
citizen of a small Greek city-state in which the gods and
goddesses of Olympus were still taken seriously, have to
say that is of relevance to education in our technological
age? With so many contemporary gurus to choose from, why
do we still hark back to Plato?

The answer: because his perception and his reasoning
power were outstanding, and he used them to wage an in-
cessant campaign in pursuit of truth - truth about the
movements of the heavenly bodies, truth about the nature
of beauty, truth in the sphere of mathematics, truth in
every sphere he could recognise, but above all, truth
about how men ought to live and conduct their lives.

Having said that, let me add at once that nobody thinks
that Plato found the truth in all these spheres. His
metaphysical speculations about a life after death do not
convince many today; his view that man can obtain moral
knowledge as certain as scientific knowledge has been
strongly contested, while some of his actual moral
values - or what are presumed to have been his values -
have provoked an almost hysterical reaction from some
critics in recent years. In addition, Plato is quite
capable of being illogical, can be seen to be gaining
points in argument on occasion by the simple device of
equivocating over the meaning of a word, and in many
celebrated passages forsakes rational argument altogether
in favour of highly emotive mythical tales.

If we bear in mind also that at least some of his
empirical claims now appear to have been clearly dis-
proven, and that much of what he says is inevitably
coloured by the beliefs and limited knowledge of the time
in which he lived, it should be clear that Plato is not
being introduced as some kind of final authority whose
words should be received with hallowed respect and un-
critical faith. His greatness lies in his astonishing
ability to raise those questions which, while they would
not normally occur to most of us, are none the less of
enormous significance; his manner of clinging ruthlessly
to such questions, refusing to take an easy way out or to
ignore them as unpalatable obstacles in the way of his
prejudices, and, despite the severe limitations acknowledged above, his relative capacity to argue his case
rationally, penetratingly and powerfully.
Many of those who know Plato's work may well disagree
with most of his conclusions; few would imagine that the
conclusions could have been arrived at by a more capable
advocate.

PHILOSOPHY PAST AND PRESENT

It is common to refer to a 'revolution in philosophy'
which took place earlier this century, inaugurated by the
work of Wittgenstein.
Philosophy today is broadly speaking understood by most
practising philosophers to consist of the activity of
analysis or the examination of meaning: a philosopher
pursues such questions as 'What constitutes indoctrination?' or 'What is it to be educated?' 'What could the
claim that God exists or that all men are equal mean?'
'In what sense could such propositions be true?' 'What
would count as evidence for or against their truth?' With
one or two notable exceptions philosophers do not regard
it as part of their function to tell people how they ought
to behave, how they ought to organise society or education,
or wherein true wisdom lies.
Plato, by contrast, devotes a great deal of space to
constructing Utopian societies, telling his readers how
they ought to live, attempting to establish not only that
there is an after life, but also that it takes a particular form, and generally taking seriously a class of metaphysical propositions that to one school of twentieth
century thought at least (the logical-positivists) are
literal non-sense.
But perhaps this distinction between analysis of
meaning and prescription for conduct is more apparent
than real, and perhaps 'the elimination of metaphysics'

(the title of a chapter in Ayer, 1936) was not in fact
the death blow to a certain kind of philosophy so much as
one more contribution to the age old debate about such
questions as whether God exists or whether there is some
absolute and eternal principle of justice. After all, to
claim as the logical-positivists did, that a statement of
the form 'this is just' cannot be true or false, since it
is really a way of expressing one's approval of the act,
does not put an end to metaphysics: it is, in one sense,
merely another move within the sphere of metaphysics. It
is one answer to the metaphysical question 'Does justice
exist?'; by implication it is a negative answer, but, of
course, it is not necessarily the correct answer - that
after all is what the metaphysical argument is all about:
are philosophers like Plato who claim some kind of real
existence for Justice in the abstract convincing or, at
the other extreme, are the logical-positivists convincing?

Similarly there is ultimately surely not a great deal
of difference between arguing that 'to be educated means
such and such or necessarily involves such and such' and
arguing that people ought to be educated in such and such
a way. For, if our concern is with the normative use of
the term education, then our analysis of the concept will
necessarily involve reference to our values. Again the
object of enquiring into the meaning and use of moral
terminology is presumably intended to throw some light on
what conduct may reasonably be regarded as worthy of moral
approval, which suggests that such analysis is merely one
means of attempting to answer the age old question 'How
ought we to live our lives?' And this technique of analysis is very far from being the discovery of this century.
Plato was the originator of it, so far as we can tell;
for those innumerable dialogues that start from a question
such as 'What is courage?' are nothing if not object
lessons in conceptual analysis (e.g. Plato, 'Laches').

In short, although there are passages in Plato that go
beyond what we would expect from an academic philosopher
today - not least because Plato was pioneering in the
fields of sociology and psychology as well - essentially
he remains an excellent example of the philosopher, even
as currently understood. By means of close analysis of
key concepts and rigorous argument he attempts to approach
some kind of answer to these elusive questions that cannot
readily be answered by appeal to the senses, consensus or
experiment.

PHILOSOPHY OF EDUCATION

Philosophers dispute the nature of philosophy of education
no less than they dispute the proper bounds of philosophy
in general. Here I only have space to assert my own view
that philosophy of education is nothing more nor less than
the application of philosophy to specifically educational
issues. On this view it is not a logically distinct
branch of philosophy, and it involves recourse to such
logically distinct branches as there are. As Hare has
observed, there can be no doubt that 'Plato was the
founder of the philosophy of education' (Hare, 1970,
vol.1, p.15) in this sense. For that is to say that the
application of philosophy to the sphere of education, the
relating of the findings of ethics, political philosophy,
epistemology and so on to education, was one of his basic
concerns - which is undeniably true.

However the combined impact of the educational view of
Plato, countless other philosophers and countless other
people, has naturally given rise over the years to new
objections and new questions. Thus contemporary philosophers of education are interested in a number of concepts
and arguments with which Plato, for one, does not directly
deal. For example, Plato's own political and educational
proposals readily give rise to the accusation that what he
advocates amounts to 'indoctrination'. Here we have a
concept that has occupied a great deal of the time of contemporary philosophers, but with which Plato does not
concern himself directly at all. (He does, of course, by
implication, effectively state that in his view it is not
indoctrination, or, alternatively, that, if it is, the
term has no pejorative implication and he is in
favour of it.) Other concepts and issues that both
interest contemporary philosophers of education and spring
readily to mind when one reads Plato (either as points he
seems to have missed or as points he seems to be making
in another way) are: autonomy, discovery learning, play,
knowledge, the concept of education itself, the question
of the degree of freedom that should be granted to
children in various respects, the notion of a liberal
education, the question of a just distribution of education, and above all, the whole issue of moral education.

My object in the following pages has been to convey
what Plato has to say about education, to relate it to his
philosophical underpinning, to examine the cogency of that
philosophical underpinning to some extent, and to relate
the whole to some of the issues, such as those mentioned
above, that concern the contemporary philosopher of education. My hope is that the pertinence of Plato today

will thus be self-evident, and that the reader will treat
this book, not as a compendium of the thoughts of a Great
Man, but as material for critical thought.

It is quite likely that much of what Plato has to say
will strike some readers as thoroughly obnoxious - there
are many aspects of his point of view which happen to rest
ill alongside the current liberal orthodoxy. He is in
many respects a challenge to that orthodoxy. But he who
shares with Plato a passion for the truth, rather than a
mean-spirited devotion to his present opinions, will know
that the challenge must be seriously examined and met by
rational argument, or else rightly judged to be compel-
ling.

OUTLINE OF THE FOLLOWING CHAPTERS

The points made above explain to some extent the format of
this book. Chapter 2 briefly sets Plato in his historical
context, since there are a number of things that Plato
says and proposes which cannot be properly understood
except in the context of his times. The view that somebody's historical background may have important reper-
cussions on some of their attitudes and beliefs is, of
course, quite distinct from the view that the validity of
a person's attitudes or beliefs is historically (or
culturally) determined, and from the view that all
knowledge is necessarily conditioned and controlled by the
pervading ethos of a particular time and place. The claim
here is that Plato has things to say which transcend the
circumstances in which he found himself, but that he was
clearly influenced by some of those circumstances in some
ways.

In chapter 3 the argument of the 'Republic' is
outlined - first the general political proposals and then
the educational programme. Exposition of the former is
necessary in that Plato's educational views are very
closely interwoven with his ethico-political views. His
educational views are not by any means expressed only in
the 'Republic', and this is not a book on the 'Republic'
exclusively. None the less that dialogue contains his
fullest statement of the principles by which he thinks we
should be governed in educational matters.

Chapter 4 considers Plato's distribution of education
and the question of whether the policy of one kind of
education for one kind of person and another for another
offends the principle of equality or justice. Chapter 5
is concerned with certain points that Plato makes about
teaching methods. In particular it is concerned to

suggest that attempts to cite Plato as the source of
certain currently popular notions is without foundation.
The remaining three chapters are all concerned with
the curriculum or the content of education. In chapter 6
Plato's theory of knowledge is examined, in chapter 7 his
attitudes to the arts, and in chapter 8 the findings of
the two previous chapters are brought together in relation
to the topic on which Plato has most to say: moral education.

Chapter two

Historical background

THE PELOPONNESIAN WAR

In 431 BC democratic Athens and her allies went to war
with the Peloponnesian League led by Sparta, which may
reasonably be seen as the prototype of a closed or
totalitarian society. The war lasted on and off for
twenty-eight years. In 404 BC the Athenians were
defeated and the democracy was replaced by a government
of thirty pro-Spartan oligarchs - known simply as the
Thirty. But even prior to the final defeat, morale must
have been severely shaken in Athens. During the first
few years of the war the city was ravaged by plague and,
with the death of Pericles, she lost a notable statesman,
whose successors, according to one contemporary source,
'were all concerned to advance themselves; they adopted
cheap political tactics and so failed to control affairs
properly; naturally many mistakes were made' (Thucydides, 'The Peloponnesian War', 2.65. Cf.Aristotle, 'Constitution of Athens', 28.1).

A series of important events illustrate a prima facie
loss of sound judgment on the part of the democracy, and
increasing tension within the city. On one day in 427 BC
the Assembly voted to put to death every adult male in
the city of Mytilene, which had unsuccessfully tried to
revolt; on the next day the vote was reversed (Thucydides, 3.36 ff.). In 424 BC Cleon who 'more than anybody
debased politics by his violent methods, ranting, raving,
abusing and insulting in the Assembly' (Aristotle,
'Constitution of Athens', 28.1) was elected from nowhere
to a generalship. He was elected, if Thucydides is to be
believed, on the extraordinary grounds that the mass of
the people thought it would be good sport to foist a
command on him that he did not really want, while 'the
more intelligent took the view that if Cleon were to

succeed that would be good for the city, and that if he
failed that would put paid to him' (Thucydides, 4.27 ff.).
In 416 BC the Athenians voted to put to death all the
male inhabitants of the island of Melos simply because it
wanted to remain neutral. Theoretically, one would have
expected it to be an ally of the Spartans (since the
Melians and the Spartans had racial ties). This time
there were no second thoughts and Thucydides records a
memorable dialogue between the Melian and Athenian repre-
sentatives, in which the arguments of the latter represent
a locus classicus for amoral cynicism (Thucydides, 5.85
ff.). Perhaps the most foolhardy of decisions was made
in 415 BC when the Athenians, by no means in a position
of strength in the Aegean, voted to open up a new theatre
of war in Sicily. The result was a catastrophic defeat
involving the loss of thousands of men. So grave was the
crisis precipitated by that defeat that in 411 BC the
democracy was temporarily suspended; for a short period
Athens was actually in a state of effective civil war,
with the oligarchs dominating the city itself, and the
democrats operating from the naval base on the island of
Samos.

In drawing attention to these events I have, of course,
been highly selective, and in cataloguing them so briefly
I have in no way done justice to their complexity. To
make but one cautionary reservation: although it is
certainly true that contemporary sources are by and large
unanimous in condemning Pericles' successors as dema-
gogues, it is also true that most contemporary sources
are the work of those who might be classified as of oligarchic persuasion.(For a full account of this matter, see
Barrow, 1973, ch.4.) However, no historian could deny, I
think, that the war years produced tension and disillusion
in Athens. To many Athenians it must have seemed that the
democratic system had proved itself incompetent to govern
wisely, and that the strain of war had had a lamentable
effect on the unifying power of those beliefs and values
that had been the pride of Athens in happier days.

SOCRATES

Socrates lived through, and Plato grew up during, the
second half of the war. Trying to disengage the philosophical views of these two men is a difficult task, since
most of what we know about Socrates comes from Plato's
dialogues (in most of which the former figures as the main
participant). But it seems reasonable to suggest that the
historical Socrates probably held the following beliefs:

that the unexamined life, or a life devoid of the questioning spirit, is not worth living; that there are certain abiding principles of conduct which should be adhered to; and that one of these principles is that one should abide by the laws of the country to which one belongs, even though one may devote one's life to arguing for their abolition.

The son of a stonemason and a midwife, Socrates, although himself trained as a stonemason, devoted most of his life to philosophy or the quest for knowledge and truth. According to some sources he was originally interested in questions that we would characterise as belonging to the natural sciences (Aristophanes, 'Clouds'). But his preoccupation soon became metaphysical subjects and, in particular, the sphere of ethics. His central concern became to examine the question of in what the Good Life consisted.

One necessary condition of living the Good Life, he became convinced, was to know oneself. 'Know thyself' was, in fact, a maxim long associated with traditional Greek wisdom, and Socrates seems to have taken this maxim over and interpreted it to mean that it is a man's positive duty to have a real understanding of himself and, in particular, to know the limits of his own wisdom. The most vivid account of this notion of self-knowledge is presented in Plato's 'Apology'. There Socrates explains how he finally came to understand why the Delphic oracle had described him as the wisest of men; by dint of questioning all the accredited groups of wise or knowledgeable men (the politicians, the poets, the technologists), he realised that without exception their pretensions exceeded their actual knowledge. True, perhaps, that Socrates did not know how to sway the Assembly with rhetoric, to compose great plays or devise useful artefacts, but what he knew, and they apparently did not, was that neither he nor they actually knew anything of great importance - such as how men ought to conduct their lives.

It should be noted that Socrates' critical attitude to the traditionally accepted authorities is not based on the claim that he knew what they did not (except specifically that he knew his own ignorance) or that they are necessarily wrong about various matters. His complaint and fear is that too many people seem to be too sure of themselves, assuming that they know what at best they have some reason to believe, and at worst lack even that. It is, therefore, arrogance or conceit in relation to belief, belief masquerading as knowledge, that he despises, and not faith or commitment itself.

This important distinction explains how it was that
Socrates, a sceptic and a questioner, could none the less
act with amazing fortitude in compliance with his beliefs.
For example, in the closing years of the war the Assembly
voted to try all the generals en bloc for allegedly
failing to ensure the safety of shipwrecked survivors
after a naval engagement. The notion of an en bloc trial
was constitutionally illegal. Socrates alone stood out
against the prevailing crowd hysteria in an attempt to
insist on the observance of the law. And again Socrates
was one of the few who dared to refuse to carry out one of
the malign orders of the Thirty (Plato, 'Apology', 32.B).

In 399 BC, when the Thirty had been ousted and the
democracy restored, Socrates was brought to trial and
condemned to death. Why is very much an open question.
Technically he was charged with impiety and misleading
the young. Some historians have argued, quite persuasive-
ly I think, that the business of bringing him to trial may
not have been as significant as we tend to imagine. It
might, for instance, have been something of a personal
vendetta between his accusers and himself, which would, in
the normal course of events, have aroused little support.
On this view the significant point would be Socrates'
conduct at his trial which, it is argued, brought conviction where it need not have done. Certainly if Plato's
'Apology' is to any marked extent a fair picture of
Socrates' defence at his trial, as it purports to be, it
is not difficult to believe that his logic-chopping, his
lack of respect for the accredited wise men of the city,
and his frivolity at such a grave moment, should have in-
furiated his more prosaic compatriots. And in support of
this thesis it may be pointed out that whereas the jury
voted by a majority of thirty votes for his condemnation,
the majority in favour of his being condemned to death was
much greater. This may be explained as a result of the
Athenian legal system, whereby accuser and accused each
proposed a penalty, one of which the jury was bound to
accept: Socrates' proposal that his penalty should be to
be fed at the public expense, then modified to a ridicu-
lously low fine, as recorded in the 'Apology', can hardly
have endeared him to the jury.

However the occasion of his being brought to trial in
the first place still needs some kind of explanation. And
it seems not unreasonable to suppose that it was at least
partly due to his questioning scepticism, which will have
struck many as disruptive, the nervous state of the restored democracy, and, above all, his associates. For his
associates did unfortunately include two members of the
Thirty and Alcibiades whom many will have regarded as the

epitome of a new breed of cynical, self-interested and
amoral young men.

Once convicted, Socrates refused to take advantage of
opportunities to escape death by going into exile. He
drank the hemlock and died true to his conviction that it
is one's duty to abide by the due process of the law of
the community when it goes against one, just as one takes
advantage of it when it offers benefits.

PLATO

Common sense insists that while Socrates must have been
affected by the events that occurred during the last part
of his life, Plato must have been strongly influenced by
those same events in his formative years. Living in a
period of physical turbulence, social disarray, and
changing values, he saw confusion, injustice, arbitrari-
ness and defeat at first hand. The treatment of Socrates
alone must have caused him to wonder about the workings
and acceptability of crowd dynamics. And it comes as no
surprise to learn that Plato's quest for Utopia leads him
to focus on the twin objectives of harmony and security.

He came from an oligarchic and wealthy family and was
a cousin and a nephew of two of the Thirty (Critias and
Charmides respectively). But it is necessary to rebut
the implication of Bertrand Russell that he was in any
way an admirer or an associate of the Thirty (Russell,
1946). Rather, as he makes clear in the 'Seventh Letter',
he was repelled by the excesses of the Thirty even more
than he had been by the incompetence of the democracy. He
writes:

Some of these men (the Thirty) happened to be relatives
and acquaintances of mine, and they invited me to join
them at once in what seemed to be a proper undertaking.
My attitude toward them is not surprising, because I
was young. I thought that they were going to lead the
city out of the unjust life she had been living and
establish her in the path of justice, so that I watched
them eagerly to see what they would do. But as I
watched them they showed in a short time that the pre-
ceding constitution (the democracy) had been a precious
thing ... I was appalled and drew back from that reign
of injustice ... At last I came to the conclusion that
all existing states are badly governed and the condition of their laws practically incurable, without
some miraculous remedy and the assistance of fortune;
and I was forced to say, in praise of true philosophy,
that from her height alone was it possible to discern

what the nature of justice is (Plato, 'Seventh Letter', 324.D).

The crucial cause of bad government, as Plato saw it, was a lack of competence on the part of the governors. Whether the governors were the people as a whole, or the few, it seemed that they did not really know what they were doing. They were not qualified to govern, and the history of political decisions in Athens was therefore largely a random business. Plato again and again reverts to the amateurish nature of politics and asks why, when we demand knowledge and skills of a specific sort in our doctors, our shoemakers and our naval captains, for example, we do not demand the same degree of competence from those who are going to steer the ship of state (e.g. Plato, 'Gorgias'). Clinging fast to what was almost certainly a dictum of Socrates - that virtue is knowledge and that people only do wrong out of ignorance - Plato finally came to the view that moral knowledge could be gained and was the necessary prerequisite of competent government. Therefore, in place of the democratic ideal of government by all for the sake of freedom, he proposed government by reason - in practical terms by the few who had the reasoning ability - for the sake of security and the well-being of all. Inevitably, then, he is drawn on to the question of education, for the question is: how are we to ensure that rational knowledge that is necessary to the ideal state is developed?

FORMAL EDUCATION IN ATHENS

Formal education in Athens during Plato's lifetime, was confined to the sons of the wealthy. Its object was to produce the 'kaloskagathos'. The term is not really translatable (literally it means 'a noble and good man'), but it conveys in a nutshell the essence of what the Athenians regarded as a cultured gentleman. The 'kaloskagathos' was physically fit and agile as a result of the physical training provided by the 'paidotribes'; he was grounded in the basic skills of reading writing and arithmetic by the 'grammatistes'. He was cultivated, which was to be defined in the terms of his familiarity with the poetic heritage and his musical ability - both the responsibility of the 'kitharistes'. He was adept in those pursuits which were regarded as indispensable to a man of leisure (notably athletics and music, but also hunting and horsemanship generally). But above all he was well-mannered and moderate in his behaviour. Most of these terms (e.g. cultivated, well-mannered, moderate),

of course, ideally require considerably more elucidation
in terms of the values of the period. But the important
point for us to note is that education is here conceived
of as essentially an initiation into a particular style
of life with a very strong emphasis on what I can only
characterise formally as proper or decent behaviour
(Plato, 'Protagoras', 325.C ff.).

THE SOPHISTS

There was nothing in the formal Athenian education to
encourage or promote what we might call intellectual
curiosity, enquiry or critical thought. If that seems
odd, when we consider the reputation that the Athenians
had for being acute and agile-minded (and when we consider
the intellectual achievements of the fifth century), it
should be remembered that the way of life of the city
itself constituted a powerful informal education. Such
critical acumen and reasoning facility as they had came
more from a daily life of discussion in the 'agora',
debate in the Assembly, and of course reflection in the
theatre, where momentous conflicts and questions were
enacted before their eyes, than from the schoolroom.

But from about the middle of the century onwards there
was an even more potent and direct stimulus to question
and examine everything from the nature of God to the ad-
visability of going to war, and that was the advent of
the sophists.

Extreme caution is needed in discussing the sophists,
because our primary source for their activities is
Plato - and, generalising, Plato was hostile to them.
Although we tend to refer to them en masse as if they
were some kind of cohesive group, they were in fact no
such thing. They were travelling lecturers, most of whom
were not Athenian but who naturally found their way there
at one time or another, since Athens was pre-eminently
the city of free speech. Another reason was that Athens,
being democratic, was the ideal state in which to lecture,
since most of the sophists claimed to teach the art of
public speaking and the way to achieve practical success
in politics by that art. Their method was to give public
lectures for high fees, and thus once again to provide
education for the rich rather than the poor.

Plato was aware of the distinction between the individual sophists. Protagoras, for instance, he clearly
regarded with some respect as an original thinker.
Hippias, on the other hand, he obviously thought to be a
conceited fool, whose proud boast that his talents were

such that everything he wore and carried had been made by
his own hands, Plato did not find particularly impressive.
Between these two extremes were those such as Gorgias who
undoubtedly had a talent for fine public speaking, judged
in terms of rhetorical flourish and style, who was not a
trivial polymath like Hippias, but whose intellect did
not compare with that of Protagoras.

Generalising (and it is a generalisation), the
sophists, with more or less ability, brought to Athens a
devastating spirit of critical rejection of the traditional beliefs and attitudes. Their radical and sceptical
questioning of the conventional moral norms and religious
assumptions contributed to a spread of nihilism and moral
relativity, which was no doubt increased by the long and
disillusioning years of war. Behind the claim to teach
the art of rhetoric lay the presumption that success in
public life, to be defined in terms of power, was more or
less the supreme achievement possible to man.

So, at any rate, Plato seems to have felt. And his
central charge against them was that, by confusing the
ability to persuade with the ability to argue a point
well, they were creating chaos and contributing to moral
anarchy and a situation in which political justice became
synonymous with political expediency. Not only were they
teaching others to identify success with virtue, but they
themselves ignorantly supposed that the identification
was valid. Thereby, according to Plato, they revealed
their basic inadequacy, which was that they professed to
teach on matters about which they knew next to nothing.
Again and again in his dialogues Plato causes Socrates to
lead some sophist (or some young man aping the ways of
the sophists) from the claim that he is in a position to
teach people about justice to a point at which it seems
that he himself is in hopeless confusion as to what
constitutes the nature of justice.

To what extent Plato's attack on the sophists is fair
is a matter of some historical interest, but is not immediately germane to our purpose. What is clear is that
the second half of the fifth century witnessed an upheaval
in respect of conventions and beliefs and that some of the
sophists contributed in no little measure to the new
spirit of questioning the accepted. But Plato had a
particular axe to grind, for, in the opinion of the many,
Socrates himself was just one more sophist, whose
scepticism could be seen as the cause of the decline of
respect for traditional values amongst the young men with
whom he associated. Plato's lifelong devotion to the task
of rehabilitating the memory of his master largely takes
the form of rebutting this popular opinion by distinguish-

ing between two kinds of critical enquiry: the good, represented by Socrates, and the bad, represented by the
sophists. In other words Plato's brief virtually makes
'sophist' a dirty word before he begins.

However, leaving aside the fairness or otherwise of
Plato's specific ad hominem charges, it is clear that he
is concerned with an important distinction. That the fact
that something is traditionally accepted as true (be it a
moral, scientific, political or religious proposition)
does not make it true, and that the proper concern of an
individual is to question and think things out for himself
are two of his fundamental axioms which he may well have
shared with some of the historical sophists. But thereafter his concern is to distinguish between what he calls
a true philosopher, whose search is for accuracy, truth
and right, with the sophist whose object is to be persuasive, effective and successful.

The task that Plato set himself was to perfect a system
of higher education that would harness the spirit of
critical questioning with the ability to do the job well -
in other words to substitute a skilled search after truth
for a trivial scepticism.

Chapter three

The`Republic´

THE POLITICAL FRAMEWORK OF THE REPUBLIC

1 Creation of a city

The 'Republic' is nominally concerned with the question
'what is justice?' Consideration of this question leads
Plato, speaking through the person of Socrates, to
outline his ideal society, as a result of which the
question of education is raised - the right kind of education being seen as a necessary condition of the
perfect society.

The task Socrates sets himself is to confute any rela-
tivistic moral thesis, such as the one put forward by
Thrasymachus in Book 1. In opposition to Thrasymachus'
claim that justice is nothing more than the advantage of
the stronger (388.C) or, as he seems to mean, that our
ideas of what is just are no more than arbitrary fiats
originally foisted on an unsuspecting majority by a domi-
nant minority, who stood to gain from the general acceptance of such ideas, Socrates hopes to show that the
nature of justice is such that a man who truly understands
it must see that it is inherently good. Whereas
Thrasymachus not unnaturally concludes from his view of
justice that, provided that one could get away with doing
all the things that are traditionally regarded as unjust,
any sane man would do so, Socrates claims that anyone who
has a true understanding cannot fail to recognise the
obligation to act justly regardless of the consequences
to himself.

What, then, is justice? It is in order to answer this
question that Plato causes Socrates to embark on the task
of outlining the perfect state. The claim is that if
some idea of what justice involves can be gained in the
larger context of society, this can then be applied to

the problem of discerning justice in the individual.
Socrates starts by envisaging a small community that
arises out of the realisation on the part of various individuals that they cannot be entirely self-sufficient and,
indeed, would positively gain from a co-operative attempt
to pool their resources. Hence a principle of special-
isation is introduced on the grounds that 'more things
will be produced and the work more easily and better done
when every man is set free from all other occupations to
do, at the appropriate time, the one thing for which he is
naturally suited' (370.C). Originally Socrates is only
thinking in terms of the various crafts: one man will
make shoes for the community, another build houses, and so
on. When it is pointed out that the society he posits is
too small and too austere to be taken seriously, he
accepts that if we are to be realistic we have to envisage
a more complex structure with a great many more crafts or
occupations. He moves rapidly to the claim that, if we
assume a fairly complex society encompassing a wide range
of activities, then we must assume that some people will
have to be concerned with the defence of the state (for it
will no longer be an insignificant community of no
interest to others) and some with the internal adminis-
tration or government. It is in this way that what Plato
calls the Guardians are introduced: they are those whose
specialist occupation is defence and control.
Just as it requires certain specific talents and abilities to be a cook, a carpenter or a cobbler, so the
Guardians will need to be specialists. Conscious of the
fact that the quality of those responsible for the maintenance, protection and smooth-running of the state is ultimately of more concern to everybody in the state than the
calibre of its cooks and carpenters, and aware also that
the characteristics of the good Guardian are less easy to
define than those of a good cobbler, Socrates now turns
his attention to the task of defining those characteristics (374.E).

2   The Guardians

He argues that good Guardians will need to have 'a love of
wisdom or truth, spirit, speed and strength' (376.C). At
the point at which this claim is made Socrates, no doubt,
still has in mind his comparison of the Guardians with
good watch-dogs who are friendly to those whom they
recognise as friends but quick to discern and challenge
an enemy. This explains the reference to the 'speed' and
'strength'. Briefly, what he seems to mean is that the
Guardians must be concerned to promote or defend what is

right and true with energy, alacrity and determination.
A more detailed picture of what is meant emerges implicitly from the detailed discussion of the education necessary
to this end, which will be dealt with below.

At the close of the section on the education of the
Guardians, Plato makes Socrates divide them into two
groups: the auxiliaries and the rulers (412.B). The
latter are chosen from the Guardians on the strength of
their ability in two quite different kinds of test.
First, they must show particular intellectual ability;
second, they must show particular concern for the
interests of the whole community or love for the state.
In other words the rulers or the philosopher-kings, as
they are called, are not simply an intellectual elite, for
they are selected by reference to a certain disposition
as well as to a certain ability (412.D). To anticipate
slightly, Plato defines his ideal ruler in terms of six
characteristics: he must be capable of abstract reasoning
about ends, capable of seeing effective means to ends,
capable of clinging to reason in the face of temptation to
do otherwise, capable of avoiding fallacious reasoning,
concerned for truth and of a benevolent disposition
(Barrow, 1974,A).

3 Communal life

Socrates now outlines the communal way of life that is to
be shared by all the Guardians. The basic idea that all
shall live together in barracks having their food
supplied directly by the largest group parallels the
Spartan way of life at that time. But Plato goes further
than the Spartans did in his total rejection of the idea
of any private property or wealth, in his proposal to
have all children brought up in communal creches from the
moment of birth, and in his inclusion of women in the
arrangements. In an important passage that indicates
that he really is concerned only with the merit of individuals, he points out that women may just as easily
satisfy the criteria laid down for picking out suitable
auxiliaries and rulers as men (455.D). If the women
amongst the Guardians are themselves Guardians they cannot
be expected to devote their time to the traditional role
of the wife at home. The notions of marriage and family
as traditionally understood by the Greeks or ourselves are
therefore totally abandoned. Children, like everything
else, are to be held in common. A complicated set of
sexual regulations are introduced partly to ensure that
only healthy children are produced and partly to guard

against the possibility of immediate blood relations
producing children from their sexual union - a situation
that could easily arise without some form of control given
that in this truly communal society nobody will know who
'his' blood relatives are. It should be noted however
that the sexual regulations are designed only to control
sexual activity in respect of producing children. Where
there is no danger of children being born anybody may have
intercourse with anyone else (458.E).

The upshot of these arrangements, Socrates claims, will
be a complete absence of possessiveness, jealousy or
private interest amongst the Guardians. The interests of
one are the interests of all. To the suggestion that the
Guardians might not like these austere conditions of
life - for not only is everything held in common, but
what is held in common includes no luxuries or re-
finements - Socrates' immediate reply is that his concern
is for the happiness of the whole community rather than
that of one group within it (420.B). The implication is
that since the state as a whole will be the better for a
body of rulers who have no opportunity for pursuing their
private interest or internal rivalries and jealousies,
whether they personally like it is of secondary importance. But, of course, he is well aware that if the
Guardians did not like their way of life the state would
never get off the ground. His real answer to the objection is that although to many of us this communal life
may appear daunting, to the Guardians, precisely because
of the sort of people they are, it will prove entirely
acceptable. Their interest lies in the pursuit of truth
and the maintenance of justice. Material pleasures are
of little or no account to them (466.A).

4   Justice

We now have three groups in the Republic: the rulers,
the auxiliaries and the largest group. With the ideal
state more or less outlined can we discern justice?
Three of the traditional Greek virtues are clearly em-
bodied in the arrangements, according to Socrates. The
state is wise in that it wisely adopts wise rulers who
rule wisely. So its wisdom is to be found in what is in
fact its smallest part, and in the fact that it gives
authority to that part. Courage is to be found amongst
the auxiliaries whose steadfastness of purpose 'preserves
under all conditions the conviction that what is to be
guarded against is whatever the lawgiver (being wise) has
laid down and impressed on them in their education should

be feared' (429.B). The city is moderate in that in
accepting the leadership of the wise the supremacy of
reasonable desires over unreasonable desires is assured.
('Sophrosune', here translated 'Moderation', is in fact a
very complex and important concept to the Greeks, which
is unfortunately done less than justice by any translation. The 'Charmides' contains a discussion on it.)

And what of justice? Surely, Socrates concludes, the
justice of this state must lie in the very principle on
which it was initially constructed, namely the principle
that each individual's role in society should be based on
what he is most naturally suited to. In other words,
'Justice is in some sense the doing of what is peculiarly
one's own' (433.B).

The final question is how this formulation can apply
to justice in the individual. Socrates argues that the
individual soul consists of three parts: reason, spirit
or determination, and appetite or desire. These three
parts correspond to the three groups in the state.
Justice in the individual, it is concluded, consists in
each of these three parts performing its proper function.
In the just man's soul reason is supreme: it governs the
whole. Determination, the equivalent of the courageous
auxiliaries, allies itself with reason and together they
control the desires. This does not of course mean that
the just man has no desires, but merely that his desires
are rationally ordered and that there is no feeling of
conflict in his soul between what there is reason to do
and what there is a desire to do.

EDUCATION IN THE REPUBLIC

1 Content of literature

Children in the Guardian group are brought up in creches
under the authority of nurses appointed by the state.
Socrates begins his account of the first stage of their
education by stressing the importance of early years in
the development of an individual: 'You realise, of
course, that in any task how one begins is the most
important thing, especially when one is dealing with any
creature that is young and tender. For it is then that
it is most malleable and takes on whatever impression one
might wish to make on it' (377.B).

What immediately concerns Plato is what he sees as the
tremendous influence of stories told to small children on
the development of their attitudes and the formation of
their character. He believes that the young are particu-

larly susceptible to example, and that they tend to
imitate the patterns of behaviour of those whom they
admire or find attractive, even if these heroes are only
fictional. 'And surely you are aware', he observes, 'that
imitations carried on from youth, gradually turn into
habits and second nature in thought, word and deed'
(395.D).

In order to understand the essence of what Plato has to
say on this subject, which largely relates to the Homeric
'Iliad' and 'Odyssey', it is necessary to appreciate that
these poems, which may appear to be no more than ossified
relics of cultural history or, to some readers, at best,
great works of literature, were of considerable significance to all Athenians - and not primarily as works of
art. The Homeric poems have often been referred to by
historians as the Bible of the Greeks, on the grounds that
they were intimately known and loved by virtually all -
including those who could not read or write, for Greek
culture was still to a large extent oral - and regarded as
a repository of the wisdom of the ages. Just as many
children in Victorian England were brought up to regard
the Bible as a handbook of religion, morality and history
rolled into one, so the Athenians regarded Homer as more
than a rich source of delightful and awe-inspiring
stories: the 'Iliad', for instance, told the historical
story of the Trojan war, showed the almost arbitrary ways
of the Gods with men, and, above all, set forth, through
the struggles of its larger-than-life heroes, a pattern of
ideal behaviour the essence of which was the relentless
passion to display one's prowess - to succeed. In an
increasingly secular age it might be more apposite to see
in Homer the Athenian equivalent of television: an all
pervasive influence that imparts a subtle combination of
information, entertainment and evaluation. It is essential in what follows to bear in mind the fact that the
Homeric poems were a potent factor in the formation of
assumptions, beliefs and attitudes for the average
Athenian.

Plato's intention is to censor this material radically.
His purge of the poems proceeds in accordance with two
principles: anything that is false and anything that
might encourage immorality or moral laxity must go. There
is nothing aesthetic about this censorship at all. The
first principle (Falsity) is directed in the main against
the anthropomorphic picture of the Olympian Gods given in
Homer. Socrates claims that any suggestion that the gods
can be responsible for evil is false; any suggestion that
the gods can change is false; and any suggestion that the
gods may deceive is false. Anyone who knows his Homer

will appreciate that cutting out such passages as perpetu-
ate one or other of these falsehoods will amount to a
sizeable piece of bowdlerising.

The primary object of this part of the censorship is,
as stated, to prevent children being taught what, according to Plato, is false. But even here he is also
concerned with the moral effect of bringing people up to
assume that such things as deception, strife and wrong-
doing are commonplace among the gods. For how can people
be expected to shrink from such behaviour, if their gods
are presumed to indulge in it? Nor will Plato accept any
defence of the antics of the Olympians based on the
suggestion that Homer is dealing in allegories. What
matters when dealing with the young is how, being young,
they will as a matter of fact understand something - not
how they ought to understand it if they were not young.

> The young are not able to distinguish between what is
> and what is not allegory, but whatever opinions are
> taken into the mind at that age are wont to prove in-
> delible and unalterable. For which reason, maybe, we
> should do our utmost to see that the first stories
> that they hear should be so composed as to bring the
> fairest lessons of virtue to their ears (378.D).

Therefore the conduct of the Homeric heroes must also be
carefully checked, and indeed any aspect of the poems
that might tend to influence children towards undesirable
conduct. Fearsome stories of the underworld, for
instance, are to be rejected on the grounds that they may
contribute to a fear of death. The excessive wailing and
lamentation of the heroes must be cut: we cannot have
Achilles self-indulgently wandering distractedly along
the shore pouring out his grief, nor Priam rolling in the
dung as he entreats the Greeks to restrain Achilles from
maltreating the body of Hector ('Iliad', 22, 414-15).
'For if our young men should take such tales seriously
rather than laugh at them as absurd, how much less likely
will they be to think such conduct unworthy of themselves'
(388.D). Plato adds further examples of what he regards
as unworthy behaviour on the part of the heroes, but it
should be noted that he is aware of the distinction
between the formal claim that bad conduct ought to be
censored and specific claims as to what behaviour is bad.
At this stage he is concerned with the formal point, and
he therefore concludes this section with the observation
that any precise account of how the poets ought to represent the behaviour of their heroes must wait upon an
adequate account of the nature of justice. When it is
clear how people ought to behave, it will become clear
how fictional characters should be presented (392.C).

2   Form in the arts

But Plato is not content with merely censoring the content
of literature presented to young children. He argues that
the form or manner in which material is presented is also
important. He distinguishes between narrative, where the
author recounts a story in his own words, and dramatic
representation, where a good speech is delivered in the
'oratio recta' of the character in question. Traditionally the Greek schoolboy was expected to immerse himself in
the character whose words he might happen to be reciting;
he was supposed to relive and express the horror of, say,
Orestes faced with the truth of his father's murder by his
mother. Socrates is opposed to this practice when the
character in question is mad, bad or merely alien to the
ideal that we wish for our children. He therefore proposes to sweep away all dramatic representation, such as
comedy, tragedy and all that is not narrative in the epic
poems, save in those cases where the character in question
is admirable. Towards the end of the 'Republic', when
Socrates returns to this theme, the demands appear to be
even stronger, for there he seems opposed to vicarious
experience of any sort. That is to say he is as sus-
picious of Homer's narrative description of a battle as
he is of his dramatic representation of Achilles' grief.
But his argument there is heavily dependent on his theory
of knowledge and will have to await our treatment of that
topic.

The discussion on the form of literature leads con-
veniently into the question of music, which would seem to
be an art peculiarly tied to form rather than content.
Here too Plato fears the effects of some music, and, in a
passage that has excited more scorn than most, argues
that we can and must distinguish between those musical
modes such as the Lydian which express sorrow and are used
for dirges and laments and which should not be used, and
those 'which will best express the accents of courage in
the face of stern necessity and misfortune, and of temper-
ance in prosperity won by peaceful pursuits' (399.A,
trans. Cornford).

Similarly those rhythms 'which are appropriate to a
life of courage and self control' are the ones to be observed.

What these rhythms are Socrates confesses he does not
actually know. And certainly it is impossible to make any
comment on the technicalities of this passage given our
ignorance of Greek music. But it is perhaps worth observing that the Greeks were disposed to reserve specific
metres and types of music for specific themes, and that

therefore Plato's remarks may not be quite as fanciful as
they appear out of context. Be that as it may, his
general point is that music can have an effect on the soul
or character of the individual. More generally, as Shorey
puts it in his excellent summary of the whole section on
censorship:

> Plato, anticipating the thought of Wordsworth and
> Ruskin, argues that the music we hear, the aesthetic
> quality of the statues, the pictures, the architecture
> we contemplate in our daily walk, the aspects of nature
> that surround our impressionable years, all tend to
> mould and fashion by silent sympathy our inner spirit-
> ual life through the sensuous organism. The true
> statesman and educator will demand that the silent,
> daily cumulative irresistible pressures of these subtle
> forces shall conspire for good rather than evil. Then
> and only then, as Socrates beautifully says, 'will our
> youth dwell in the land of health, amid fair sights and
> sounds, and receive the good in everything; and
> beauty, the affluence of fair works, shall flow into
> the eye and ear like a health-giving breeze from a
> purer region and insensibly draw the soul from earliest
> years into likeness and sympathy with the beauty of
> reason (Shorey, 1965, p.171).

3 Gymnastics

That concludes Plato's comments on 'mousike', which to the
Greeks includes both what we would call music and literature. But he accepts the traditional Greek dualism of
'music for the soul and gymnastics for the body' (376.E),
at least in so far as he includes gymnastics or physical
training, which Socrates now proceeds to discuss, in his
curriculum.

When he writes about gymnastics, Plato does not indulge
in the sort of idle speculation that one sometimes comes
across today suggesting that movement or dance may furnish
a way into forms of knowledge or that they should be
geared to the teaching of geography. Plato's concern is
quite simply to produce healthy bodies. This is partly
because he regards it as desirable in itself to be
healthy, and partly because - and this is the point at
which he deviates from the traditional Greek view - he
regards a healthy body as conducive to a healthy soul and
inner self. Those who are exclusively devoted to gymnastics, argues Socrates, and who neglect the things of
the mind become boorish and brutal; but those who are
exclusively bound up with intellectual pursuits become

'softer than is good for them'. The ideal is the mean
between these two extremes, and gymnastics therefore has
a part to play in stimulating the spirited element of the
soul; but its effects must be counterbalanced by the
musical education.

So much for the first stage of education, which must be
understood to include a basic grounding in literacy and
numeracy: Plato advises us to avoid compulsion in these
early studies but rather to approach them through play,
but such prima facie advanced methodology should not blind
us to the fact that this stage is one in which 'feelings,
opinions and habits undergo a discipline necessary for
social life, but in which there is no real attempt to open
up to the mind the completest expansion of which it is
capable' (Bosanquet, 1900, p.14).

4   The higher education

At the age of twenty, after a two year period of military
training, those who give evidence of their competence and
suitability in the tests already referred to, move on to
the higher education. This consists, first, of ten years
devoted to the study of arithmetic, geometry, astronomy
and harmonics. The purpose of this programme of studies
is primarily to give a rigorous training in abstract
thought, far removed from the categorisation and collection of actual sights and sounds in the everyday world.
This training Plato regards as an indispensable preliminary to the final stage of education to which the most
able proceed at the age of thirty. This final stage is
the study of dialectic, which, supplemented by practical
experience of life in various subordinate administrative
posts, is supposed to culminate, by the time the students
reach their fiftieth year, in the vision of the Good.

What is all this about? In a word: knowledge. The
object of the higher education is the acquisition of
knowledge both for its own sake and for its utility value
when it comes to governing and administering the state.
By dialectic Plato means philosophy as he conceives it
should be, perhaps specifically rather than as it is
practised by such pseudo-philosophers as the sophists.
It is 'a study such as philosophy would be if it fulfilled
its best aspirations as an insight into the most important
matters of life, knowledge and religion' (Bosanquet, 1900,
p.15).

And the vision of the Good? At this point I can do no
better than to quote Shorey, although both dialectic and

the vision of the Good will require further examination in
subsequent chapters.

The consummation of it all is described poetically as
the 'vision of the idea of the Good' (540.A) - which,
however, ... turns out to mean, for all practical
purposes, the apprehension of some rational unified
conception of the social aim and human well-being, and
the consistent relating of all particular beliefs and
measures to that ideal - a thing which can be achieved
only by the most highly developed intelligence (Shorey,
1935, vol.2, p.xl).

Chapter four

The distribution of education

THE CONCEPT OF EDUCATION

Peters has argued that 'education' is a normative term:
it 'implies that something worthwhile is being or has been
intentionally transmitted in a morally acceptable manner'
(Peters, 1966, p.25). But this is a purely formal point:
it says nothing about what is worthwhile or morally acceptable. Peters himself then went on to argue, more
contentiously, I think, that analysis of the notion of an
educated man showed that education also logically involved the transmission of knowledge, which, he further
claimed must not be inert and must involve cognitive per-
ceptive. In a celebrated passage he wrote

We do not call a person 'educated' who has simply
mastered a skill... For a man to be educated it is
insufficient that he should possess a mere know-how or
knack. He must also have some body of knowledge...
Some understanding of principles for the organisation
of facts... Some understanding of the 'reason why' of
things. The Spartans, for instance, were militarily
and morally trained. They knew how to fight and they
knew what was right and wrong... But we would not say
that they had received a military or moral education;
for they had never been encouraged to probe into the
principles underlying their code (Peters, 1966, p.30).

It is clear that on any view such as Peters' the majority
of the citizens in the Republic are not educated, for
knowledge is not transmitted to them (in Peters' sense of
knowledge or Plato's). Rather they are imbued with right
opinion as indeed are the auxiliaries ('Republic', 429.D):
the object behind selecting the auxiliaries and educating
them in music and gymnastics, says Socrates, 'was to con-
trive influences whereby they might take the colour of our
own institutions like a dye, so that, in virtue of having

both the right temperament and the right education, their
convictions about what ought to be feared and on all other
subjects might be indelibly fixed' (430.A).

However it would be a mistake, I think, to conclude as
some have done that the masses are so much human cattle
to Plato, that they do not interest him and that he does
not wish to educate them (Popper, 1966). For whoever the
'we' are who, according to Peters, would not call the
Spartans educated, it is evident that Plato is not one of
them. He specifically refers to the 'paideia' (education)
of the majority more than once (414.D, 420.D). And it is
an obvious inference that some aspects of the primary
stage of education outlined for the Guardians must apply
to the majority too. For if the city is to exhibit the
virtues of moderation, and if the governed must therefore
consent to the rule of the philosopher-kings, the majority
must share at least the moral upbringing of the Guardians.
It is therefore a reasonable surmise that the education in
'mousike' and gymnastics is common to all.

It would be idle to deny that for Plato the education
of philosopher-kings is in some sense superior, but, if I
am right, he must be taken to dissent from Peters' view in
this important respect: he does not see the link between
education and knowledge as conceptual. Rather he conceives of more than one kind of education, and thinks that
each of the three groups of citizens in the Republic is
being educated in a manner appropriate to it. His fundamental point, summarised in the maxim that it is unjust to
treat unequals equally, is that there are discernible
differences between children that justify different kinds
of education. And implicit in his procedure is the claim
that an upbringing that is not ultimately concerned with
knowledge so much as with right opinion may be characterised as education, and may be a sufficient and desirable
education for some.

TREATING UNEQUALS UNEQUALLY

It does not seem profitable to pursue the specific
question of whether there is reason to accept Plato's view
that the education he provides for the majority is an adequate education, in view of the fact that he says virtually nothing about it explicitly. In the remainder of this
book I shall be concerned with what he has to say about
the education of the philosopher-kings. But it is worth
taking up the basic postulate that justice demands that we
treat unequals unequally.

As it stands the principle is, of course, formal - it

says nothing about what constitutes inequality - and, in considering it, it is important to rid our minds of alleged specific concrete instances of its application and various contingent facts about such instances. One might argue that the tripartite system advocated by the 1944 Education Act is an instance of the application of this principle. But, even if it is, acceptance of the principle does not necessarily and automatically lead to acceptance of that system, since there may be other valid and important objections to it. For example, it might be argued that implementation of the tripartite system leads effectively to the classification of some as second class citizens in socio-economic terms. This consequence is contingent; it happens, or may happen, to arise in our society because of the nature of that society. Such a contingent consequence, if regarded as objectionable, may constitute a good argument against the system (or the nature of society), but it does not show that the principle on which the system is based is itself unacceptable.

Plato concludes his satire on democracy in the 'Republic' with the ironic remark that 'it really seems a most delightful form of government, with lots of variety and anarchy, distributing a kind of equality indiscriminately to equals and unequals alike' (558.C). What he is objecting to, as is clear from the context, is the notion of treating all people the same in all matters without consideration for particular circumstances and differences between people. And what he is demanding instead when he asks for unequal treatment of unequals, is that in so far as there are differences between people (i.e. they are unequal) these differences should be taken into account, and, if they prove to be relevant differences in respect of the distribution of something specific, they should lead one to treat people differently (i.e.unequally).

The claim that it is just to treat unequals unequally is thus equivalent to the claim that treatment ought to be impartial. For the principle of impartiality is the principle that people should be treated the same except where there are relevant grounds for not doing so. And that this principle is, as Plato claims, a fundamental part of justice is surely indisputable. (For a fuller explication of the principle of impartiality and the argument supporting the claim that one ought to proceed impartially, see Peters, 1966.)

NATURE/NURTURE

However, even if we accept the formal principle that it is
just to treat unequals equally, there is a real problem in
trying to apply it to educational distribution, essentially because, even if we were to agree that certain differences between children were relevant differences in
respect of education, some of these differences at least,
it might plausibly be argued, are not innate but actually
created by education.

Plato argues that a difference of what he calls
'nature' is a relevant difference. By 'nature' he means
the individual's interests and abilities: an individual
is said to be naturally suited or suited by his nature to
those tasks an understanding of which he picks up easily
and does not forget (455) and which he would freely choose
to engage in (537) and does so with competence. Of course
Plato is only concerned with a broad division between the
nature suited to a communal life and an academic curriculum and the nature suited to a practical curriculum and a
non-communal life. But although, as it happens, we might
reasonably claim that one could distinguish between
various adult natures in those respects, it does not
necessarily follow that the same distinction could have
been made in childhood or that the adults necessarily had
to turn out as they have done. Are we to say that an
individual is born with a distinctive nature or that he
acquires it through nurture and the environment?

Plato's answer to this is not very clear. He does tend
to write at times as if he believed that individuals are
born with an innate nature which is permanent. For
instance, he seems to suggest that initial classification
in one group or another can take place at birth, and some
of his references to subsequent transference from one
group to another, for which he does allow, could be taken
to imply only that mistakes might have been made at the
initial classification rather than that people's natures
might change as time passed. On the other hand this view
of Plato as one committed to the view of an unchanging
innate nature is clearly not the whole story. The whole
tenor of the 'Republic', with its stress on the power of
education to transform, makes it clear beyond a shadow of
a doubt that he believes in the potency of environmental
influence and in the efficacy of deliberate nurture to
develop a particular kind of nature.

It seems that we must attribute to Plato the view that
both nature and nurture have a part to play. Thus he
would be claiming that hereditary factors do play a part
at least in determining the likelihood or the potentiality

of an individual nature to develop in one way or another.
But this potentiality needs the right kind of nurture if
it is to be realised. In some cases, perhaps, the innate
potentiality will be so strong as to realise itself in
almost any conditions; in others the potentiality may be
so indeterminate that the nature of the environment in
which it grows will decide the issue. But in most cases
it is a question of a continual spiral of reinforcement
between the hereditary potentiality and the nurture
provided.

Whether Plato's view, if this is his view, is correct
is of course a psychological question to which I am in no
position to offer an informed answer. But perhaps one may
be forgiven for feeling that psychologists themselves are
not really in a position to give a clear and unanimous
answer. Unfortunately the question of whether education
is justly distributed in the Republic seems ultimately to
hang on the question of how significant nature and nurture
respectively are.

CLASS SOCIETY

Plato's hostile critics have made great play with the
charge that the Republic is a class-society in the sense
that it is a society in which what the individual does,
what rewards he is entitled to, what privileges he is
allowed, and so on are decided by his parentage or the
class into which he is born. It should by now be clear
that Plato did not think that it was or intend it to be a
class-society in this pejorative sense. He states clearly
that the nature of the individual rather than his birth
should be the criterion for deciding what type of education he should pursue, and hence what kind of social
role he should ultimately fulfil (374.C). And he explicitly says that if, for example, the child of Guardian
parents should appear more suited by nature to the education and way of life of the non-Guardians he should be
transferred, and vice versa (415.A).

However some critics have argued that, whatever Plato
intended, the arrangements of the Republic are such that
it must effectively turn into a class society in the pejorative sense. Thus Rankin suggests that 'Plato wanted
mobility of talent within society but (the) assimilative
tendencies in his society are against it... people become
what they do. They become what they perceive. They are
therefore liable to be fixed in the group in which they
were born' (Rankin, 1969, p.76). In other words the
suggestion is that such is the distinctive nature of the

different kinds of upbringing allotted to children, and
such is the tendency of those upbringings to mould, that
it is unlikely that in practice any child would be transferred from one group to another. Being born the child
of Guardian parents would tend to cause one to be initially classified in the Guardian group: being brought up as
a future Guardian would tend to ensure that one did indeed
develop a nature suited to that occupation. Thus, in
effect, though not by Plato's intention, parentage would
dictate the future social role of the child.

This line of argument seems to me to be well founded,
although it is important to stress that it is based on the
empirical claim that the significance of innate factors in
an individual nature is negligible compared to the significance of the nurture provided - a claim that is not,
in fact, clearly and unambiguously verified. We therefore
have to conclude that in so far as this empirical hypothesis is sound, the distribution of education in the
Republic is not in fact equitable or just. For although
we accept the formal principle that unequals should be
treated unequally, and although we agree that innate
differences of nature could be relevant grounds for pro-
viding different kinds of education to different people,
there seems little reason to accept the view that there
is a marked innate difference between natures, and none
at all to accept a system which, regardless of the honest
intentions that produced it, in fact amounts to offering
different kinds of education on the criterion of birth.
For surely we should agree that one's parentage is not in
itself a relevant reason for distinguishing between people
in respect of education.

Chapter five

Methodology

LEARNING BY DISCOVERY

There is a famous passage in the 'Meno' in which Socrates
leads a previously untutored slave to the knowledge that
in order to construct a square double the area of a given
square it is necessary to construct it on the diagonal of
the first square, rather than by doubling the length of
its sides. Having drawn a square two feet by two feet,
Socrates asks: 'How long will the side of a square twice
as big as this one be?'
Slave: 'Twice as long, obviously.'
Socrates: 'Note that I am teaching him nothing, Meno,
only asking. He thinks that he knows how long the side
of an eight foot square must be, but does he?'
Meno: 'Of course not.'
Socrates: 'Now watch how he recollects things in
order, as it should be done. (Turning again to the
slave.) According to you a line double the length of
the original line will produce a square twice as big as
the first. Is that still your view? ... Very well,
then, if we add another line of the same length to the
first, will the new line be double the length?'
Slave: 'Yes.'
Socrates: 'Alright, then if we construct a square on
this line, we should, on your view, get one twice the
size of the original square.'
Socrates then proceeds to draw the square, and, still by
means of questions, he leads the slave to see that what he
has now drawn is in fact a square four times as big as the
original one. In the final stage of the demonstration
Socrates draws in the diagonals of the four squares of
original size that go to make up the sixteen foot square,
and asks how many segments there are half the size of the
original square in the newly formed central square. The

slave correctly answers four, agrees that four is twice
two, and that therefore the square is twice the size of
the original.

Socrates: 'On what line have we constructed this
square?'
Slave (pointing):   'This one.'
Socrates: 'The one which goes from corner to corner
of the original square?'
Slave: 'Yes.'
Socrates: 'That line is known as the diagonal. So
your view is that the square on the diagonal of the
original square is double the size of the original
square?'
Slave: 'Yes.' (Plato, 'Meno', 82.B ff.)

According to Socrates, Meno will agree that the slave dis-
covered the truth without being taught. He (Socrates)
himself gave no instructions or explanations, but merely
asked questions. Was Plato, then, one of the first to
advocate discovery methods of teaching?

Certainly we have here an example of learning by discovery in some sense. But, as Dearden points out in a
concise paper, one of the main purposes of which is to
argue that discovery learning and instruction are not incompatible - 'Instruction needs to be supplemented, not
supplanted' - we have to be careful to distinguish different senses of learning by discovery. He distinguishes
three senses which he labels the pre-school model, ab-
stractionism and 'problem-solving'. And he argues, con-
vincingly in my view, that discovery learning in either
of the first two senses is inadequate as a prescription
for method (Dearden, 1967). But Socrates' experiment with
the slave is, as Dearden again points out, an example of
discovery learning in the sense of problem solving.

The teacher concerned with discovery learning in this
sense provides material which he sees as suitable to some
specific end, he knows what end he has in mind, and he
guides the child to a perception of that end. Thus he
might provide children with a variety of cardboard
triangles, show them how to use a protractor, suggest that
they measure the angles of each triangle and thereby lead
them to discover for themselves that the angles of any
triangle add up to 180 degrees; he might further ask them
whether they have noted anything about the angles of all
the right angled triangles, or again whether there is any
notable feature common to the isosceles triangles. The
hall-mark of this approach is that, though the teacher
does not tell the children the answer, he does tell them
the question or questions that require answering.

> This kind of discovery is not a romantic sailing forth
> into the unknown on a journey which will bring who-
> knows-what ecstatic joys and thrills, nor is it the
> illumination of the soul by an intellectual grace which
> somehow proceeds from apparatus. The teacher does not
> 'provide experiences' but guides experience, by the
> subtle use of language, towards learning something that
> is regarded as educationally valuable (Dearden, 1967,
> p.151).

And certain points, well illustrated by Plato's example,
must be stressed. First, the teacher does have to know
what he is doing: Socrates could not have directed the
slave in any meaningful way had he not known what the
solution was, what he was looking for and, hence, when and
in what way the slave was going wrong at certain points.
Second, Socrates is a trifle disingenuous, and he misleads
when he claims that he is not 'teaching' but only prompt-
ing by means of questions. Of course he is not teaching
if we define teaching exclusively in terms of talking or
announcing information. But such arbitrary and re-
strictive analyses of the concept of teaching, which lead
some to say that education can take place without teaching, do little or no good. They merely tempt the intel-
lectually inept to assume that children left with material
and their own wits will automatically gain something of
educational value from the experience. But any plausible
analysis of the concept of teaching will surely recognise
that it is a polymorphous activity. As Hirst puts it,
'Manifestly teaching is no one specific activity readily
identifiable in general circumstances like, say, walking
or running or riding a bicycle. There are an enormous
number of specific activities which may, in fact, be
teaching' (Hirst, 1973, p.165). One of which I submit is
Socrates' procedure here. Third, it should be noted that,
in any case, Socrates does, as a matter of fact, need to
'tell' or 'instruct' even in this example, for he wishes
the slave to learn the term 'diagonal'. This is not as
trivial a point as it may seem, for although the final
piece of information is not necessary to the purpose of
the slave seeing that the square on the diagonal is double
the original square, it is necessary to the further and
surely equally important purpose of his being able to com-
municate with people who share this knowledge.

Finally this method of teaching inevitably requires the
most careful guidance on the part of the teacher.
Socrates may not happen to do much telling or instructing,
but he certainly steers the slave with considerable per-
sistence; had he not done so the slave would presumably
have stopped at the point at which he wrongly imagines
that he has the right answer (Plato, 'Meno', 82).

WAS PLATO AN ADVOCATE OF DISCOVERY LEARNING?

Granted that Plato here illustrates a specific kind of discovery learning, was he in fact advocating that method? The example is introduced in the middle of a discussion about the nature of virtue in order to make a point about Plato's metaphysical beliefs and, incidentally, his theory of knowledge. Plato believed in a corpus of absolute knowledge such that the truths of mathematics and indeed other disciplines were fixed and eternal. (This will be discussed in greater detail in the next chapter.) He also believed in the transmigration of souls. According to this doctrine, when some person died his soul departed to another world where all things became known to it. It was then reborn in another body. But the body encloses and blinds the soul as well as houses it, so the newborn baby appears to have no knowledge. In reality, however, the knowledge is there, innate in the soul, and all that is required is some stimulus to bring it forth. (The reader may care to consider how this theory fits in with Plato's views on 'nature'.)

This is the metaphysical theory that lies behind Plato's dictum that education consists of turning the eye of the soul in the right direction ('Republic', 518.C). It also explains the example in the 'Meno'. For what Plato is concerned to demonstrate is that the slave actually knows the mathematical proposition that he finally arrives at. Hence Socrates refers to him 're-collecting' various points rather than 'learning' or 'discovering' them.

Presumably few readers will be inclined to accept this doctrine of recollection, involving as it does a claim about eternal souls and another world, without considerable qualification. Its importance from our point of view is that it warns us against reading too much into the example as evidence for Plato's educational views. It has not been sufficiently observed that Plato is not necessarily advocating this method of teaching. He is not necessarily making any value judgments. All that he is necessarily claiming, so far as his educational views go, is that this is one method whereby the child (or any un-tutored person) may be brought to acquire knowledge. (He does incidentally use the example to illustrate one other point that is part of his educational theory, namely that learning cannot take place until false conceit has been replaced by awareness of one's ignorance. It is not until the slave reaches the stage of realising that he does not know the side of a square of eight feet, not until he feels honest perplexity, that he is in a position to learn the truth ('Meno', 84.A).

It is of course a further question, and one that cannot
really be pursued here, as to whether there is good reason
to claim that Plato or anyone else should have advocated
discovery learning. But a few brief comments on this
question may be in order.

That such an approach to learning may have its ad-
vantages over the didactic imparting of information from
the motivational point of view seems a plausible enough
claim, though we are perhaps too ready to accept on
slender evidence that children do not like having things
explained to them. Conversely it is surely indisputable
that this method cannot seriously be advocated as the sole
desirable method of teaching. In the first place, some
basic instruction would surely have to take place in such
matters as the meaning of terms, the use of material and
so on. Second, there is not time to cover the ground that
there is reason to think it desirable to cover by this
relatively time-consuming method. Third, the method seems
clearly more suited to some spheres of knowledge than
others: specifically it seems more suited to those areas,
such as mathematics and science, which are characterised
by some fairly clear and determinate answers and which
lend themselves readily to validation through direct perception, at least at a basic level, than to spheres of
human activity such as the study of literature or history.

The crucial question would seem to be whether there are
good grounds to accept the claim that this way of ac-
quiring knowledge is superior in some way to other methods
such as straightforward instruction.

It might, for instance, be suggested that learning by
this method involves enquiry, and that a spirit of enquiry
is necessary to all learning. Thus the method could be
commended on the grounds that it teaches the child how to
learn. But this argument is weak in as much as the spirit
of enquiry is not exclusively the outcome of practice in
problem solving, and it is not in any case true that it is
necessary to learning: one can learn without enquiring
after knowledge. Nor does there appear any convincing
evidence that practice in problem solving in a particular
sphere, say mathematics, generates any greater capability
in problem solving in any other sphere, such as biology.
Nor would one expect it to since these two spheres are in
various important respects quite distinct. Presumably
practice in problem solving in a particular sphere such
as mathematics may lead to increased competence at problem
solving in that sphere; but so might increased mathematical knowledge imparted by instruction. Again it might be
claimed that knowledge acquired through discovery will be
better learned in the sense that it will be better retain-

ed or in the sense that the knowledge thus acquired will
not be inert or merely a collection of empty formulae and
propositions - words to be reiterated without compre-
hension. But there seems little concrete evidence to
support such claims, and no obvious reason why instruction
and straightforward demonstration should not be employed
in such a way as to achieve the same objectives.

To sum up: Plato is aware of the sense of discovery
learning that Dearden characterises as problem-solving.
There is no reason to suppose that he would have approved
of discovery learning in any other sense. Nor is there in
fact any evidence that he advocated problem-solving as the
best way to teach. There does not appear to be an over-
whelming case for regarding problem-solving as a markedly
superior way of teaching. It seems rather that it is one
of many methods all of which may have their place. And
that, I believe, is the most that Plato would have claimed
for it.

PLAY

It may perhaps be felt that I have been too hasty in
playing down the significance of the 'Meno' example for
Plato's educational views, in view of what he has to say
about the importance of play in early education. In a
notable passage, he writes:

> All this study of arithmetic and geometry and all the
> preliminary studies that are indispensable preparation
> for dialectics must be presented to them while still
> young, not in the form of compulsory instruction,
> because a free man ought not to pursue any study
> slavishly... Nothing that is learned under compulsion
> stays in the mind. Do not, then, keep children to
> their studies by compulsion, but by play. That will
> also better enable you to discern the natural capa-
> bilities of each ('Republic', 536.D).

A number of complex and sometimes extravagant theories of
play have been produced over the years. By a theory of
play I mean simply a theory about the function or significance (or both) of play. Examples of such theories might
be Froebel's view that through play the child reveals and
unfolds the essence of his nature or Lane's similar view
that in play the child displays his power and original
goodness which subsequently become distorted or perverted
by the restrictions imposed during upbringing.

One problem with many such theories is that it is not
always clear precisely what its author means by 'play'.
A second and equally important problem with any such

theory is the status of the theory itself. What reason is
there for accepting it? What kind of evidence would count
to establish or refute it? It seems fairly clear that
theories of play are generally on the plane of metaphysical doctrines for which there is not and cannot in the
nature of things be any evidence sufficient either to
establish or to refute them. Certainly this is the case
with the theories of Froebel and Lane: how on earth could
one establish that the nature revealed in play is the
individual's 'essential nature', except by making it true
by definition? And the dogma of original goodness, like
its traditional counterpart original sin, seems no less
untouchable. The claim is not that such theories are
necessarily false, but rather that it is impossible to
establish whether they are or not. This is a problem, of
course, which theories of play share with many other
psychological and sociological theories that we are unfortunately too often inclined to accept as established
facts.

The point to make here is that although Plato is
sometimes quoted as a source and authority by play-theo-
rists he does not really offer anything worthy of the name
of a theory of play. Nor, it must be admitted, does he
make it very clear what he means by 'play'.

He seems to have two concerns only in respect of play.
First, to make use of 'play' in the sense of 'the activities that children spontaneously choose to engage in for
their intrinsic pleasure' as a guide to the nature of a
child, which it will be remembered, is necessary to his
intention to allocate children in one of the two groups
according to their nature. And second, to make learning
as enjoyable as possible by making use of 'play' in the
sense of 'games'. Thus, he refers, with approval, to
Egypt

> Where lessons have been devised in ciphering for mere
> babes-in-arms which they can learn with a good deal of
> fun and amusement, problems about the distribution of
> a fixed total of apples and garlands among larger and
> smaller groups... They have a game in which they dis-
> tribute mixed sets of saucers of gold, silver, copper
> and similar materials... in this way they incorporate
> the elementary application of arithmetic in children's
> play (Plato, 'Laws', 819.B, C).

But despite these points, particularly the first, it would
be a mistake to see Plato as an advocate of anything ap-
proaching a play-way style of education or as a believer
in placing any great emphasis on children's freedom to
pursue whatever activities they might spontaneously
choose. True, he claims in the passage quoted that

'nothing that is learned under compulsion stays in the
mind'. It is conceivable that with a very precise and
restricted definition of 'compulsion' one might argue
that this is true and that Plato believed it. On any
normal definition it is palpably false and Plato did not
believe it. That this is so can clearly be seen from a
passage in which Socrates warns that because people tend
to regard play as inconsequential they fail to see the
importance of music, which they classify as a form of play
or relaxation, in education. He does not challenge the
identification of 'mousike' with a form of play, but
instead challenges the view that being a form of play it
is harmless or irrelevant. Hence he specifically demands
that the young must join in a more law-abiding play,
since, if play grows lawless and the children likewise,
'it is impossible that they should grow up to be men of
serious temper and lawful spirit' (Plato, 'Republic',
424.E). And the notion that Plato seriously meant there
to be a distinction between play, which would be free and
desirable, and compulsion which would not, is exploded by
his statement that

> When it is ensured that the same children should always
> play the same games in one and the same way, and get
> their pleasure from the same playthings, the regu-
> lations in more serious matters are free to remain un-
> disturbed. Whereas (he adds, when children are left
> to play as they like, setting their own standards of
> prettiness, attractiveness and pleasure), Society can
> face no worse evil (Plato, 'Laws', 797.A).

The truth is, as anyone familiar with the 'Laws' or the
'Republic' must know, that far from desiring to reinstate
play (in the sense of activity freely chosen by the child
for its intrinsic pleasure) at the centre of education,
Plato wishes to a considerable extent to subject even play
to his iron discipline. The acceptability or otherwise of
his proposal to turn every aspect of the child's environment into a force for Good will be considered in the final
chapter.

FREEDOM

As far as the treatment of children at what we would call
the primary and secondary stage goes, there are clear
indications that Plato wanted it to be humane and concerned for their welfare. His remarks on play and the
patience that he attributes to Socrates in his lesson with
the slave indicate that, as does his theory of punishment
which is essentially reformative. Plato wants children to

enjoy what they are doing, he does not want them roughly
bullied and threatened, and he does not subscribe to the
view that some misdemeanour on the part of the child
automatically justifies some retaliatory penalty.

But the fact remains that their education is to be
superintended and controlled by the adult population - to
be precise the philosopher-kings. He wants them to enjoy
what they learn, but they will in no way decide what that
should be. He does not slip from the proposition that the
child should be treated as an end in himself to the claim
that the child should therefore determine the path of his
own education. One of the fundamental axioms of Plato's
thought is that only one who has full understanding of
something himself can be qualified to teach it, and this
carries the corollary that in an ideal situation there
must be an unbridgeable gulf between teacher and taught:
the teacher has knowledge and it is that knowledge that
entitles him to control the course of education. Or
perhaps we might say that it is the knowledge itself that
must dictate the path of learning.

It is true that Plato himself claims to be an advocate
of freedom, but he can only get away with this claim if we
accept his rather unusual positive conception of freedom
as being free to do what reason demands. If to be master
of oneself, in the sense of the rational part of one's
soul having control of the other parts, is to be free, as
Plato maintains ('Republic', 431.B), then he is, of
course, a champion of freedom. If on the other hand
freedom is taken more prosaically to involve doing what
one feels like doing, regardless of the state of one's
soul, it must be admitted that Plato scorns such an ideal
('Gorgias', 467.A, 'Republic', 577.D).

So far as children are concerned he clearly takes the
view that their freedom, in the conventional sense, should
be limited extensively by reference to moral demands and
the more general demands implicit in the type of education
that reason dictates.

DIALECTIC

When the stage of higher education is reached the situation changes. Now teacher and taught must advance together. True learning at this advanced level, he maintains, cannot take place with books or mere instruction.
Books, he argues, cannot talk back; books cannot amplify
a point, correct the reader when he has misinterpreted a
passage, correct themselves in response to the reader's
argument or bolster an argument that turns out to have

been inadequate. True advancement in learning requires
the free give and take of face to face discussion or of
'dialectic', and this, of course, explains the usual
format of his own writings: the dialogue form
('Phaedrus', 275.D).

Dialectic originally meant little more than the art of
conversation. For Plato, although he is seldom very
precise about its meaning, it meant considerably more than
mere discussion without qualification. In the first place
he seems to have reserved its use for discussion relating
to the world of Forms or Ideas, especially the Idea of the
Good. To make essentially the same point without reference to the Theory of Forms we may say that Plato taught
the application of philosophy to the moral, political,
social and religious spheres of life. A little more
precision can be given to this by referring to two of the
techniques of dialectic practised by Socrates in the dialogues: 'elenchus' and 'epagoge'. 'Elenchus' is the
technique of causing a man to drop or revise his original
statement by leading him in the course of questioning to
accept as an ultimate consequence of it a statement
contradicting it. 'Epagoge' consists of causing another
disputant to accept a generalisation by getting him to
agree to a series of instances.

Perhaps, finally dialectic defies accurate description:
it is that which Plato creates in his dialogues. It is
the ruthless pursuit of some problem, the search for truth
on some matter conducted with determination, subtlety,
precision and care. It eschews short cuts, debating
points, and persuasive arguments. It involves a genuine
dialogue between two persons concerned not to 'win' but
to lose something of their own ignorance. This for Plato
was the coping stone of education. It is to dialectic
that his students are finally introduced after being prepared for it by study and practice in the close consecu-
tive thinking in the abstract sciences of maths, astronomy
and physics.

With his conception of dialectic Plato strikes a
radical blow against any view of education that sees it
ultimately in terms of facts to be stored, the mindless
accumulation of obiter dicta or the passive reception of
unquestionable fiats. And superficially there is a resemblance between his picture of the student of dialectics
and such currently popular conceptions as lateral-think-
ing, divergent or open-ended thinking and crap-detecting,
for all have in common a distrust of and objection to the
idea of students' blind and unquestioning acceptance of
the dictates or judgments of tradition and authority.

But in the end, the resemblance probably is only superficial, for Plato's advocacy of dialectic is very carefully qualified. First he is emphatic that dialectic should
be reserved for the final stage of education. We do not
perhaps have to take the precise ages that he sets for
various stages of education to begin too seriously. But
we do have to take seriously the basic point that in his
view the rigorous questioning that constitutes dialectics
cannot profitably be enquired into except by those who
are competent in the art of philosophising, and that art
cannot be acquired without prior hard schooling in the
business of abstract thinking. 'Every precaution must be
taken in introducing people to dialectics', observes
Socrates.

> One chief safeguard is not to suffer them to taste of
> it while young. For I'm sure that you have observed
> that, young men, when they first get a taste of dispu-
> tation, misuse it as a form of sport, always employing
> it contentiously... They delight like puppies in
> pulling about and tearing with words all who approach
> them... and when they have themselves confuted many
> and been confuted by many, they quickly fall into a
> violent distrust of all that they formally held true;
> and the outcome is that they themselves and the whole
> business of philosophy are discredited ('Republic',
> 539).

Second, while demanding this process of learning through
free discussion between equals, Plato in no way sub-
scribes to any such view as that we should be 'interested
in students' developing their own criteria or standards
for judging the quality, precision and relevance of ideas'
(Postman and Weingartner, 1971, p.44). That the students
involved in dialectic should submit their own views on
the question at issue is one thing; but that they should
also be the arbiters of what criteria they use for as-
sessing the validity of their argument for that view is
quite another. The student of dialectic is not subject
to the authority of any teacher, but he is subject to the
rule of reason: he goes not whither he will, but whither
the argument leads him.

Plato feels that the consummation of education should
be knowledge. Since he takes knowledge to be correct
opinion secured by sound reasoning, this means that his
notion of the fully educated man is not one who has meekly
imbibed a lot of information and opinion, but one who by
examination and questioning sees for himself that such and
such is the case. In this demand that the individual
should ideally refuse to accept the truth of propositions
simply because they are conventionally regarded as true he

is, of course, at one with the sophists. But the sophists
then fallaciously move to the conclusion that, because
tradition does not make something true, personal conviction does, and from the premise that certain things
traditionally assumed to be true are not known to be true,
to the conclusion that they are not true. But, says Plato
in effect, the matter is just not as simple as that.

The truth is that the important and complex questions
facing mankind - questions such as how to live, how to
organise states, whether there is a God and all questions
of value - demand not only information but considerable
skill in abstract reasoning and understanding of various
logically distinct forms of thought, of complex concepts
and fundamental principles. What he fears is a world
tainted with sophistic displays of verbal virtuosity, a
world in which people who lack the necessary competence
and who are wedded to the superficial appearances of
things arrogantly stumble towards ignorant solutions to
these momentous questions.

Chapter six

Curriculum   I Knowledge

Central to Plato's philosophy is his theory of knowledge
and it lies also at the heart of the Republic. The final
stage of the education of the philosopher-kings is almost
exclusively concerned with knowledge, culminating in the
acquisition of knowledge of the Good through dialectic.
It is because they have this knowledge that they are fit
to rule; it is because they have this knowledge that
they can distinguish right opinion or correct belief from
incorrect belief and hence superintend the implanting of
the former in the minds of the young; and it is because
Plato has an unwavering commitment to the notion that the
cosmos is a rational whole which can be understood that
he can posit the ideal of philosopher-kings: people who
know the truth in all spheres including the moral sphere.
The basis of his theory of knowledge is thus that there
is an objective truth in all spheres and that it can be
known.

THEORY OF FORMS

Before considering this basic tenet of his theory of
knowledge it is necessary to outline the theory of forms
or ideas.

Plato argues, surely correctly, that knowledge must be
of what is. One cannot know something that is false and
one cannot know something that is uncertain or changing.
The false or what is not is the object of ignorance, and
the uncertain is the object of belief or opinion. Thus
in everyday terms, I may properly be said to know that a
fruit cake weighs three pounds, assuming that it does and
that I have weighed it; but I cannot properly be said to
know that it is delicious, for deliciousness, being a
matter of taste, is variable, uncertain or changing and
hence is a matter of opinion or belief.

However we are not going to remain with everyday terms and examples for long, because, according to Plato, the entire physical world that we perceive is manifestly a world of change and uncertainty. Things are not what they seem.

A stick placed in water looks different to the same stick out of water. A landscape will look different in different weather conditions, from different standpoints or simply to different eyes. One man seems tall compared to another, but short compared to a third. An action seems right in one set of circumstances, but wrong in another. Seeds grow into flowers and trees, babies into adults. Rocks change their shape with the passage of time and the ravaging of the weather. Even the fruit cake may become lighter as it becomes staler.

On the basis of such reflections Plato concludes that the physical or material world, the world we inhabit which some may call the real world, is not in fact real at all, but rather a world of shifting appearances. There is nothing fixed and immutable about the world as we see it and therefore the world as we see it cannot be the object of knowledge. Only 'what is' can be known, and what we perceive around us is not 'what is' so much as the changing appearances of 'what is'.

So where is reality to be found? Where is 'what is'? If what we perceive is merely a variety of appearances of the stick, for example, where is the stick itself: the true stick that is, as opposed to the various manifestations of the stick. Plato's answer is to posit a world of forms or ideas. Any actual physical entity, such as a bed, or a specific activity such as returning a sum of money entrusted to one is an imperfect manifestation of some form or idea which alone has reality. It is imperfect because it is corrupted by the physical world of appearances. We give the name bed to a host of more or less dissimilar objects in view of something about them which is not directly perceived but which constitutes their essential bedness. This essential bedness is the idea or form of bedness. Similarly, acts such as returning money entrusted to one may be examples of goodness, but they are not goodness itself. Goodness itself, the form or idea of goodness, is that which is essentially common to all specific examples of good actions in the physical world: they are good in that they partake of the form of goodness. True knowledge, therefore, is knowledge of the world of forms or ideas, for only they are constant and unchanging. New designs may come and go for beds, but there is an idea of bedness, an essential bedness, that goes on for ever.

CRITIQUE OF THE THEORY OF FORMS

What are we to make of this? Some have found great diffi-
culty in doing more than scorning the theory of forms for
its metaphysical pretensions. Where, they ask, is this
other world of forms supposed to be? What does it mean
to talk of the existence of another world of ideas that
is more real than the world we inhabit? And they conclude
that the bed in the sky is little more than pie.

It is quite true that Plato himself did seem to believe
in the actual existence of the world of forms in some
sense. In the 'Phaedrus', for example, he quite explicitly claims that every human soul has seen the form of
justice prior to its rebirth in a human body. And whatever such a passage is taken to mean it clearly involves
attributing transcendental reality to the ideas. However
we do not have to be troubled by the metaphysical issue.
For it is absolutely clear that for practical purposes the
theory says something that can be understood and needs to
be taken seriously, whether or not we accept the metaphysical trappings.

What is important is the claim that specific instances
of any thing or type of action, although they will invariably differ in some respects, are linked by a common
essence. It is in view of this common essence that they
are grouped together and true knowledge is dependent on
grasping the essence and not being misled by the vari-
ations in appearance of the particular examples.

Thus to know what a bed is it is not sufficient to be
familiar with a bed; it is not even sufficient to see
that this particular bed is a bed. It is necessary to
appreciate in virtue of what it is a bed or, in other
words, what the essence of all beds is. When one knows
that one knows something; up until that point one merely
has, at best, the correct opinion that various objects
are in fact examples of bedness.

In point of fact Plato is not particularly interested
in the application of the theory of forms to concrete
notions such as that of bed. He introduces them, generally, in order to explain the theory, and it is by no means
clear whether his final position involves positing ideas
for everything from mud to justice. He is primarily concerned with the realm of abstract notions, such as
justice, good and piety. The core of the theory of forms
is therefore the view that true knowledge about such
things as piety is dependent upon getting beyond the
limitation imposed by concentrating on particular examples
of (allegedly) pious acts and arriving at an understanding
of what is essential to any act that is correctly to be

termed pious. It is, in other words, at least a demand
for what we now call conceptual analysis.

It is certainly true that Plato himself assumes there
to be an essence or form of, say, piety such that piety
just is such and such and anybody who used the word in a
different way would be misusing language. A number of
philosophers take exception to this assumption, preferring
to face the fact that some words just are used in different ways by different people. But for practical purposes,
I suggest, this difference of perspective is not crucial.
For what Plato might quite reasonably argue is that any
individual, if he really knows what he is talking about,
must have a clear conception of what he takes to be the
form of whatever he is talking about. The objection to
a character like Euthyphro (who claims to know what acts
are pious in the dialogue named after him) remains that,
though he refers to specific actions as 'pious', he apparently does not know why he does so: he does not have
a coherent account to give of piety itself. Evidently
Plato believed that if we all examined the concept compe-
tently and in depth we would all recognise its one true
and essential nature. But if we do not see any reason to
accept that, we surely must accept that if two disputants
really thought about what they meant by 'piety' and
offered coherent but different accounts they would in
fact be talking about different things; and Plato might
reasonably conclude that they each have their eye on a
different form. His fundamental point is that informed
debate on any matter demands the ability to give a clear
account of whatever form or forms are referred to.

PLATO'S THEORY OF KNOWLEDGE

It must be stressed that in reducing the theory of forms
to a stress on the need for conceptual analysis, I am
undoubtedly ignoring metaphysical beliefs which Plato did
hold. With that caution in mind Plato's argument about
the nature of knowledge might be summarised as follows:

The cosmos is the product of a divine rational mind;
all things cohere and all things may in principle be
known. But knowledge about the true condition of the
world does not consist in, and will not be acquired by,
the mere accumulation of experience and observation. On
the contrary, such direct perception may positively lead
one into ignorance. Even on a simple level what directly
presents itself to our senses will not in itself give us
knowledge. One begins to know something about a bed when
one begins to appreciate something about its function;

the path towards such appreciation is paved by abstraction - abstracting the defining or essential characteristics of 'bed' - which is to say conceptual analysis.
To really know about beds involves recognising separate
instances of bed not as a result of familiarity with such
instances but as a result of knowing the form, which
cannot come from observation alone. For unless one
recognises the form, one has no way whereby to decide
whether various instances are really instances of bed.

On a more complex level questions about God, morality,
politics and aesthetics, for example, demand a high level
of abstraction for their resolution. One does not observe
that God exists, one does not know that a picture is
beautiful simply by perceiving it, one does not find the
truth about morality by collecting observed instances of
moral behaviour. Things are not what they seem. The way
to get behind and beyond appearances is to hypothesise,
examine and reason, always looking to what is essential
to the concept or concepts in question. What is meant by
'God' and by 'existence'? What is it about this particular good act that makes it good? What is the beauty
itself in virtue of which we call this particular picture
beautiful? If we knew the answers to these kind of
questions then we should have more than belief (true or
false) as to the question of whether this particular act
is good or that particular painting beautiful. For we
should know what goodness and beauty themselves were and
hence would be in a position to make informed judgments
about particular instances.

THE LINE AND THE CAVE

Plato claims that only knowledge of the forms is true or
real knowledge. But by means of the diagram of the line
(509.D) he does distinguish three other modes of cognition. At the lowest level there is 'eikasia' which can
only be inadequately translated as conjecture or imagi-
ning. Those whose awareness of life remains at this level
are the sort of people who take even illusions or second-
hand reports at their face value: to them reality consists of precisely what is presented to them. One stage
above this is belief which at least attempts to distinguish between what is really there to be perceived and
what only appears to appear. Together 'eikasia' and
belief constitute the world of appearances and the realm
of opinion.

Next we move over the shadow-line that divides the
world of appearance from the real world, which is to say

the world of intelligence. And the next stage up Plato
calls 'dianoia', by which he means abstract thinking of a
sort, but the sort exemplified in such disciplines as
geometry where the abstraction triangularity, for
instance, which is reasoned about is not wholly divorced
in the mind from concrete (and imperfect) instances of
triangles. Those who, by education, can be introduced to
this mode of cognition are not deceived by appearances.
They have the ability to reason at least within systems,
such as the mathematical. But the basic axioms of the
system itself they do not question. To have true
knowledge involves getting outside of various disciplines
of thought themselves and by reasoning about the pure
forms to arrive at an understanding of the very premises
on which other systems of thought or disciplines are
based. But this true and complete knowledge is dependent
on knowledge of the form of the good.

This schematic approach is then given flesh and blood
in the parable of the cave to which the reader is referred
since no paraphrase can do it justice (514.A).

Plato's basic point that perception alone cannot give
us any knowledge worth the name is surely correct. A
perception may well be accurate or true, but if we are
exclusively wed to perception we should have no way of
knowing that it was. There is a need to escape domination
by particulars and appearances and to indulge in abstract
thought. To simply observe X, or, to be more accurate,
have the impression that one is observing X, will not
increase one's knowledge in any meaningful sense if one
cannot hypothesise, categorise, abstract, deduce and
reflect. And again Plato is surely correct in his fundamental claim that to point out instances or examples of
beautiful things, good actions and so on does not in
itself constitute real knowledge of beauty or goodness.
Real knowledge involves being able to give an account of
why things are as they are. Why is this painting beautiful? What is it about this painting that makes it
correct to describe it as beautiful? These are the sort
of questions that a man who knows beauty should be able
to answer.

Furthermore there is, I suggest, something in Plato's
distinction between 'dianoia' and true knowledge which is
of the forms. I take him to mean something like this:
competence in such rational disciplines as sociology,
history, mathematics or whatever, betokens an acute mind
on the level of 'dianoia'. But the findings of such
disciplines do not constitute real knowledge until their
fundamental axioms and their crucial concepts are examined
and understood. The most obvious and persuasive example

of this point occurs in relation to psychology which is a
discipline that proceeds in a rational manner on the
basis of certain postulates and hypotheses to tell us
about human nature. But whether its findings represent
true knowledge depends not only on the validity of the
reasoning within the discipline but also upon the truth
of the basic assumptions. That, Plato is effectively
saying, is a matter for dialectic or philosophical enquiry. He is thus implicitly putting forward the idea of
what we would call philosophy of psychology, philosophy
of science, philosophy of history and so on. Philosophy
he sees as the science of sciences, knowledge of systems
of knowledge, or, as we phrase more or less the same
thought today, a second-order activity. (The same thought
is canvassed in the 'Charmides'.) And surely he is right
to do so. Logically the ultimate and hence fundamental
questions just are philosophical: we cannot reasonably
treat the findings of, say, Freudian psychology as known
truths without examining the status and validity of its
basic premises, and such an enquiry would be philosophical
in kind.

IS KNOWLEDGE ABSOLUTE?

But even if the reader accepts my defence of Plato so far,
this still leaves two crucial questions: is Plato correct
in claiming that in all matters there is a truth which can
be objectively known? And in particular, what exactly is
the function of the form of the Good in Plato's theory?
By the claim that a proposition is true I mean simply
that it corresponds to or describes an actual state of
affairs. By knowledge I mean, in company with most contemporary philosophers, but in Plato's words, correct
opinion tethered by a chain of reasoning ('Meno', 97.E).
In modern terminology that is to say that there are three
conditions, which taken together are necessary and sufficient conditions of knowledge: 1 the proposition one
claims to know must be true; 2 the one who claims to
know the proposition to be true must believe it to be
true; and 3 he must have evidence for its truth.
It is clear that given that this is what 'true' and
'knowledge' mean certain currently fashionable slogans,
such as 'the truth is as you see it' or 'truth is culturally determined', are at best misleading and at worst
false. The truth is not as you see it: if the cat is on
the mat, i.e. if the proposition 'the cat is on the mat'
describes an actual state of affairs - namely the fact
that the cat is on the mat, then the proposition 'the cat

is on the mat' is true, whether you can see it or not.
Similarly the suggestion that there can in principle be
no such thing as objective knowledge (which seems to lie
behind some of the more extreme assertions of the view
that knowledge is relative), is evidently false: if the
cat is on the mat, if we believe the proposition, 'the cat
is on the mat' to be true, and if we have the evidence to
establish the truth of the proposition, then we have
knowledge, and that knowledge is not to be identified with
a subjective opinion.

However this establishes only that given the meaning of
the terms 'true' and 'knowledge' there must in principle
be such a thing as objective knowledge. But how in fact
can we ever know that our claims to knowledge are true?
Certainly I can in principle know that the cat is on the
mat, but how in fact can I know that it is on the mat,
rather than that I am the victim of, say, some hallucin-
ation? The problem arises out of the evidence criterion
of knowledge: how do we know in any given instance that
our evidence is good enough? Certainly if the evidence
of my eyes does not deceive me, then I know that the cat
is on the mat and that knowledge is by definition a matter
of objective fact. But how do I know that my eyes do not
deceive me? How do I know that the evidence I have is
sufficient to establish my claim?

Now I think we may reasonably say that, although a
genuine problem is raised here, with simple propositions
such as 'the cat is on the mat' it seems in general absurd
to question the validity of the evidence. We should agree
with Plato that for all practical purposes the evidence is
sufficient and it therefore makes sense to claim that we
can know the truth of such propositions.

But Plato wants to claim far more than this. According
to him we can know not only that the cat is on the mat,
but also that God is in his heaven, that beauty consists
in such and such or that the true nature of justice is
such and such. These claims however raise a real problem
about evidence. For what kind of evidence would establish
whether God exists or not or what is truly just? Whereas
few would seriously dispute that the evidence of our eyes
is sufficient to establish the truth of the proposition
'the cat is on the mat' there is genuine and widespread
disagreement about what kind of evidence, if any, would
be sufficient to establish the truth of such propositions
as religious, moral or aesthetic propositions. And this
disagreement cannot reasonably be ignored. It is all very
well for Plato to say that serious dialectics will reveal
the truth on such matters, but how, when we are discussing
the question of God's existence, are we supposed to tell a

good point from a bad one, if we have no basic agreement ·
on the sort of evidence that would be relevant to the
question?

So even if Plato is right in his claim that there is
in principle a truth to be found in all matters and all
spheres - and I suppose in some sense he must be right:
even a proposition such as 'God exists', as some people
normally intend it, must be either true or false. Either
God exists or he does not, so there is a truth, whatever
it may be, even on this issue - none the less his notion
that the truth can be known in all spheres, whether
through dialectics or anything else, cannot be accepted
as it stands. There are some spheres of human enquiry at
least where talk of knowing the truth or the answers seems
inappropriate, because we do not agree on what would count
as evidence to establish the truth of propositions in
these spheres. We cannot accept that the philosopher-
kings or anybody else will come to know whether God exists
or that this picture just is the most beautiful in the
world.

Is this a crippling blow to Plato's whole argument? I
don't think so. For the essence of his view may be pre-
served if we substitute some such notion as 'informed
opinion' for knowledge in these spheres, where we do not
think the attainment of absolutely certain knowledge is
possible. Though we may say that nobody knows whether God
exists or not, we can still distinguish between those
whose opinion on the matter is governed by appearances and
those whose opinion is based on reflection and understanding of the problems inherent in the matter, and the kind
of reflection required would be, as Plato maintains, dia-
lectical or philosophical. It is only by asking questions
like what could the claim that 'God exists' possibly mean,
in what senses could it be true, what kind of evidence
would be sufficient to establish or refute the claim, that
we can hope to have an informed opinion on the matter.
But of course our informed opinion may very likely be the
view that the truth in this matter is beyond our grasp.

From the political point of view this modification to
Plato's theory of knowledge may have significant reper-
cussions: if the philosopher-kings have only informed
opinion and in some important spheres know only that
certain knowledge is not possible, it may be felt that
the only grounds for their absolute rule have been swept
away. This interesting question cannot unfortunately be
pursued here. But from the educational point of view the
modification makes little difference. Plato would still
argue that the object of his higher education must be to
lead students towards truth and knowledge, the modifi-

cation being that on some matters the knowledge acquired
would be knowledge of our ignorance and uncertainty. He
would still argue that the art of abstract thinking and
looking beyond particulars and appearances must be cultivated. And he would still argue that the ultimate study
must be dialectics or philosophy: the study of the basic
hypotheses of other disciplines and the logical status of
their findings and the search for the true nature (which
might become the search to see whether there is a true
nature) of such abstract concepts as justice, beauty, and
truth and knowledge themselves.

THE IDEA OF THE GOOD

The idea or form of the Good stands as the goal of higher
education and to know it is to have attained the summit
of knowledge. Plato refused to give a written account of
the nature of this supreme form. The most he was prepared to do was provide the analogy with the sun from
which some have inferred that Plato is claiming that
knowledge of the Good automatically leads to an understanding of the unity of all knowledge - it brings together as it were the disparate disciplines. This may be
so, but, if it is, it seems to be at a variance with the
'Charmides' in which dialogue Plato seems to distinguish
between the science of sciences (i.e. philosophy) which
welds the branches of knowledge together, and knowledge
of the Good (i.e. moral philosophy) which does not reveal
the unity of all knowledge so much as give point or
purpose to it. In the 'Republic' he also offers obscure
hints about the relationship between the various forms
(a relationship not without problems as he himself ap-
preciated in other dialogues). According to some
scholars he claimed that all forms were somehow dependent
on the form of the Good; according to others, whom I
prefer to follow, it is only the various moral forms that
owe their existence to and are revealed by the light of
the Good.

Now I do not wish to deny that here again Plato undoubtedly does mean a lot of obscure and mysterious
things. But arguing about the metaphysical status of the
idea of Good must not blind us to one simple sommon sense
thing that he is undoubtedly saying: namely that moral
philosophy is of supreme significance. Dialectics must
ultimately concern itself with moral questions. As he
says quite simply in the 'Euthyphro', for example, the
differences between people that really matter and demand
our most urgent attention are 'differences of opinion as

to what is good and evil, just and unjust, honourable and'
dishonourable' ('Euthyphro', 7.E). These are the differences that cannot easily be resolved by observation or
experiment, and these are the differences that set men
against one another. Furthermore not only is the moral
sphere of supreme practical importance for this reason,
but as Plato also unambiguously implies throughout the
dialogues, there is no particular point in knowing
anything if we do not know what we ought to do about it:
to know how to make money, how to be popular, how to
manufacture bombs, etc., is all grossly irrelevant if we
do not know whether it is good to do this or that.

The significance of the idea of the Good then lies at
least in these mundane considerations. But, of course,
Plato believes that here, no less than in all other
spheres, absolute knowledge of goodness is possible. The
question of what this view, which we can no longer accept,
means for his programme of moral education I shall defer
to the final chapter.

THE IDEAL OF A LIBERAL EDUCATION

In his article Liberal Education and the Nature of
Knowledge, P.H.Hirst refers to 'the fully developed Greek
notion of liberal education', presumably with Plato in
mind (Hirst, 1972, p.391). He argues that the Greek conception of a liberal education was governed and justified
largely by the presumption that complete and absolute
knowledge was attainable in all spheres. Given that few
today would accept that presumption he seeks to outline a
new version of an education that would involve development
of the mind and liberation from error. And the basis of
his conception of a liberal education is to be found in a
new understanding of the nature of knowledge. According
to Hirst there are a certain number of logically distinct
forms of knowledge or ways of understanding experience,
and initiation into these forms would constitute a liberal
education.

It is, I think, reasonable to conclude that Plato
today, if he were to accept the modern view that absolute
knowledge is not obviously attainable in all spheres,
would approve in principle of an approach to education
such as Hirst's. That is to say, he would approve of the
ideal of initiation into whatever forms of knowledge there
are. Where he might take issue with Hirst, however, is,
first, on the question of what logically distinct forms
there are and, second, on Hirst's implication that philosophy is merely one form of knowledge on an equal footing
with others.

But he surely would agree that the ideal education is
concerned with the development of mind and that this means
cultivating an understanding of whatever forms of
knowledge there are, culminating in an understanding of
the philosophical form of knowledge.

Chapter seven

Curriculum 2 Art

A THEORY OF BEAUTY

In the 'Laws' Plato suggests that a work of art has three
aspects that require consideration: its charm or propensity for giving pleasure, its technical merit and its
propensity for producing good or bad effects ('Laws',
667.B ff.).
The technical merit of a work is exhibited in the
internal harmony of the constituent parts of the work.
It is clear that by 'internal harmony' Plato means, at
least, to refer to such straightforward matters as harmony
in music and proportion in building, sculpture and
painting. (See, for example, 'Symposium', 187.) Thus
'regular curves, rhythmical repetitions, symmetrical
figures are all instances of harmony' (Crombie, 1962,
p.189). But he seems to mean rather more than this in
passages such as the following:

> The Muses... would never commit the grave mistake of
> setting masculine language to an effeminate scale, or
> tune, or wedding melody, or postures worthy of free
> men with rhythms only fit for slaves and bondsmen, or
> taking the pose of a free man and combining it with an
> air or words of inappropriate rhythm... (But in the
> works of our poets) not only do we see confusion of
> this kind, but they go still further. They divorce
> rhythm and movement from melody, by giving metrical
> form to bare discourse, and melody and rhythm from
> words, by their employment of cithern and flute
> without vocal accompaniment ('Laws', 669.C).

Beyond sensing that this is a demand for something more
than mere musical harmony, I confess to having no real
understanding of what Plato is talking about here. And I
doubt whether we can profitably do more at this stage than
acknowledge that we do not know precisely what Plato means

by 'internal harmony' in this context. (Would Plato have
thought that the paintings of Picasso's blue period had
internal harmony or the compositions of Bartok? I see no
way of answering the question.) Thus essentially we have
no more than a formal claim from Plato to the effect that
a song or any other work of art is well wrought or
displays technical merit in so far as it consists of what
is suitable, internally consistent or harmonious. There
is insufficient evidence to attempt to fill out this
formal claim with a coherent account of Plato's substantive view of what such harmony or suitability might
involve in any specific art form.

The property of charm or giving pleasure is not of
course peculiar to art. But there is reason to believe
that Plato was working towards a theory of aesthetic
beauty that would define the concept in terms of both the
pleasure and the technical merit in a work, such that the
beauty of a work would be dependent on the pleasure af-
forded by the harmonious arrangement of its constituent
parts. The notion that beauty is some kind of pleasure
is first introduced in the 'Hippias Major', although all
the specific proposals, such as that beauty is what gives
pleasure through sight and hearing or that it is harmless
pleasure, are subsequently rejected. But in the
'Philebus', which also takes up again the idea that due
proportion and seemliness are essential to the technical
merit of a work, the connection between beauty and
pleasure is reintroduced with an important modification.

The discussion centres on true pleasures, which for
Plato means pleasures that are pleasant in themselves
rather than, for instance, in that they involve a relief
from pain. For example a sweet taste is pleasant in
itself, whereas a drink of water may only give pleasure
because a man is suffering from thirst. As another
example of a true pleasure Socrates cites 'those which
are given by beauty of colour or form' ('Philebus', 51.B)
and he goes on to stress that he is not referring to
such things as the beauty of a face as it appears in a
painting but to the beauty of the composition itself,
which is to say the beauty inherent in the arrangement of
the lines, the circles and the colour. This seems clearly
to suggest that for Plato beauty in art may be defined in
some such way as 'the propensity to produce pleasure by
means of harmonious composition'. Thus we may say that
aesthetic appreciation consists of appreciating the
beauty of such things as tonal shape, linear form or
colour pattern, which appreciation is evidenced by the
pleasure one feels in contemplating them.

This, of course, is still formal, for true aesthetic
appreciation or appreciation of what is genuinely beautiful will depend upon a true awareness of which tonal,
lineal or colour arrangements deserve to be regarded as
harmonious. The nearest that Plato came to saying
anything specific and comprehensible about what sort of
works of art actually do possess this beauty is in the
'Republic' (399-402), to which the reader is referred.
But it should be added that he may not find it particularly helpful. The only point that comes out very
clearly in that passage (and elsewhere in the dialogues)
is that Plato sees a tight correspondence between having
the ability to discern true beauty and having a virtuous
soul. The good man or the just man, it will be remembered, is one whose soul is harmoniously attuned with his
desires and whose passions willingly accept the control of
reason. This internal harmony in the good man is the
guarantee of his awareness of the need for and the nature
of harmony generally, hence it is his judgment of aesthetic beauty, and not that of some character whose soul
is in turmoil, that counts.

ASSESSING THE VALUE OF A WORK OF ART

But, according to Plato, it is the third aspect that is
all important. So far he has been talking of what beauty
is (or pursuing the form of beauty), and in what a well-
wrought work of art would consist. But when it comes to
appraising the value of a work of art the aesthetic
criterion is insufficient; we must look to its propensity to promote good or ill. It is true that by
identifying true beauty with beauty as perceived by good
men Plato seems to have run the aesthetic and moral criterion together. But he does seem to allow the possibility of works of art that have aesthetic merit and yet
are morally neutral (see 'Laws', 667.E, 653.D); and his
whole treatment of Homer in the 'Republic' implies
strongly that the poems are great works of art but morally
suspect.

Be that as it may, it is absolutely certain that in our
terms Plato is arguing that the question of the moral
influence of a work takes priority over the question of
its aesthetic merit. (See for example, 'Republic', 401.B).
Any notion of art for art's sake is hereby totally rejected. It is conceded that if a work is morally neutral
but has charm it may serve a useful purpose in that it
provides relaxation and pleasure ('Laws', 653.D). But if
there is any chance of it being morally corruptive its

charm is irrelevant. Thus we cancel various passages in
Homer, although they are acknowledged to be 'poetic and
charming' to most people ('Republic', 387.B). Another
passage ought to be expunged, although it is granted that
it may well give 'pleasure' ('Republic', 390.A). We may
adore or respond to the poet of 'subtlety and charm', but
we must reject him in favour of the less charming poet
'who would imitate the diction of the good man' and teach
the moral lessons we approve ('Republic', 398.A). And
the better the poet technically, the worse the danger of
his influence.

Two points are worth stressing at this juncture.
First, Greek literature was primarily didactic and, with
few exceptions, from the time of Homer, through the
corpus of lyric and elegiac poets in the seventh and
sixth centuries, to the Attic tragedians and historians,
it concerned itself with pointing moral lessons or making
moral judgments. And not only was it didactic in nature
but it was literally taken as to some degree authoritative on such matters. But besides writing in a world
in which such figures as Homer, Sophocles and Euripides
were taken seriously as moral authorities, Plato's
tendency to evaluate works of art ultimately by reference
to their moral content seems also to be typically Greek.
For example, the so-called literary contest between
Euripides and Aeschylus in Aristophanes' comedy the
'Frogs' to see which of them is the better poet, is not
really about literature at all. Despite the contrary
view of many classicists, it is clearly a contest to see
which is the most desirable didactic writer - to see
which of the poets is the best in the sense of likely to
offer the most beneficial advice and guidance to the
Athenians. Aristophanes himself more than once tells us
that the poet's job is to teach. And even that classic
of literary criticism, Aristotle's 'Poetics', is remarkable (to us) in that its evaluation of Greek tragedy is
virtually unconcerned with what we should call purely
poetic or aesthetic considerations. Aristotle cate-
gorises six constituent parts of a tragedy - its plot,
character, thought, diction, spectacle and song. It is
in discussing diction that he gets nearest to what we
might regard as purely aesthetic considerations. But
diction, by which term Aristotle means to refer to such
tricks of the trade as vivid metaphor and the use of un-
familiar words, is ranked as of least importance in the
constituent parts of a good tragedy. It is transparently
clear that what really matters to Aristotle are the plot,
the character and the thought. A good tragedy, to him,
is essentially one that has an edifying story to tell and

tells it effectively, the character and the plot being
important in that it is necessary that they should be
credible in order to convey the edifying moral contained
in the thought.

Second, Plato was no philistine. We do not have to
believe the story that he himself was a writer of trage-
dies, which he burnt on meeting Socrates, to appreciate
that. We have the evidence of his dialogues which few
would deny (even without the assurance of knowing the
form of beauty) to contain some literary masterpieces.
Nor should we be misled by his rough handling of the
artist in the 'Republic'. It is true that he expressly
expels all poets by the end of the work - he does not rest
content with a mere censoring of Homer - but there is an
unmistakeable wistfulness about his stressing that if
someone can successfully plead their case against him (in
prose) so much the better. His admiration for artists,
such as Homer, as artists is quite clearly expressed at
many points. He even goes so far as to picture them as
divinely inspired. And his interest in questions of pure
aesthetics is abundantly witnessed by such dialogues as
the 'Ion', the 'Philebus' and the 'Hippias Major'.

His fundamental objection to artists is that they pose
as, and are taken to be, what they are not. It is the
fact that they are revered as sages which troubles him.
The poet writes about things about which he does not know
and is taken to be an authority on matters about which he
is basically ignorant. True knowledge can only be acquired through study of the forms. Only the forms are
real. The everyday world of sense-experience is one
remove from reality. But the artist, dealing as he does
in representations of the sensible world, which are themselves merely representations of the ideal forms, is two
removes from reality. He is trafficking in imitations of
imitations. And yet this is the man, one can hear Plato
exclaiming, to whom we are supposed to listen and whose
opinions subtly infiltrate and mould our own.

It seems to me that, if we can once again get beyond
Plato's metaphysical language at this point, we see that
he is saying something of considerable interest and
possibly something that needs to be taken seriously. I
shall confine this discussion to the literary artist.

OBJECTIONS TO THE LITERARY ARTIST

The literary artist deals in form and content. The form,
if it is well handled, may constitute a most seductive
influence upon the reader: the charm and technical

expertise of Homer, regardless of precisely what they involve, draw the reader to take him seriously. But what
does Homer write about? About the gods, about warfare,
about human relationships, human conduct and other such
intricate and momentous questions. Now what does Homer
know about these things? Qua artist he knows nothing;
qua artist he knows only how to tell the tale well.

According to the theory of forms, as I have interpreted
it, to make informed comment on such matters it is necessary to have considerable ability in abstract thought and
conceptual analysis. To know about warfare requires, besides practical experience of, and accurate information
about war, reflection on it and above all consideration
of such key concepts as courage, cowardice and war
itself. Similarly to talk with understanding about the
gods presupposes philosophical reflection on the nature
of the gods, the plausibility of claiming they exist, and
so on. Above all there is the ethical content, which can
never be hidden for long, which, if it is to derive from
knowledge rather than the mere opinion of the author, presupposes contemplation of the form of the Good or, more
prosaically, the study of moral philosophy.

Of course Homer, or any other author, may as a matter
of fact be more than merely an artist. If this is the
case, if he happens also to be a philosopher and to have
thought in the right way about such issues, then these
strictures would not apply to him. But even here Plato
would oppose the notion of the artist's work being an
entirely desirable medium for revealing his own knowledge
to others. For the manner of his presentation is not
conducive to enhancing the understanding of the reader,
since it does not involve straightforward rational argument or discussion.

In a modern context, the argument appears to be something like this. Our ultimate aim is to bring about true
understanding of the world and its various aspects, particularly of the moral sphere. Thus, for example, we should
like people to have a true understanding of courage rather
than that they should have some hazy notion of courage as
perhaps 'being tough' or 'putting the boat in'. Courage
being a normative term it is particularly important that
people should not think that, say, brutal terrorising
necessarily involves courage. (In order to allow for the
objection considered in the previous chapter that there
is not one true form of courage, one could rephrase this
to say that people ideally should examine the concept of
courage philosophically to see whether they really feel
that what they previously took to be 'courage' necessarily
is.) Now it so happens that certain literary artists,

such as Joseph Conrad, are particularly drawn to the theme
of courage. If Conrad, besides being a great literary
artist, has something of the philosopher about him, his
work will at least present a true picture (or an informed
picture) of courage. To that extent he is preferable to
those writers who show no signs of being able to offer any
rational account of the themes with which they deal. But
there is still a problem, because such is the nature of
story-telling that we cannot by any means be sure that
what Conrad actually means to convey will come across to
the reader; and in any case, assuming that it does, this
gives the reader only an example of courage. It does not
bring him to an understanding of why this is an example of
courage; it does not involve grappling with the concept
itself.

Of course, it would be unrealistic to expect young
children at least to be able to indulge in the philosophical analysis or the dialectic ideally required. This
presumably explains Plato's inconsistency between Book 3
of the 'Republic' where he merely wants Homer censored,
and Book 10 where he appears to want all poetry excluded
from the city. Perhaps we may say that ideally he wants
adults to eschew the seductive pleasure of poetry and
concentrate on rational discussion. But that he realises
that children need first to form some conception of e.g.
courage before they can talk about it; he is therefore
prepared to countenance the use of literature provided
that it enshrines 'right opinion'.

APPLICATION OF PLATO'S ATTITUDE TO THE ARTS

Here then is a serious challenge to the view that literature (or the fine arts in general) are a potent medium of
teaching. They may have their place as influences for
the Good, if they enshrine right opinion. But they do
not represent a path to true knowledge. For the path to
knowledge is paved by the mastery of concepts and rational argument, not by the seductive form of art.

It is, of course, very difficult to apply Plato's
attitude to art to modern circumstances. For example, in
introducing prose fiction I have already gone beyond what
Plato actually says, since he was not familiar with that
particular art form. Given the enormous variety and complexity of art forms today compared with the situation
with which Plato was familiar, given that we may not see
reason to share some of his substantive moral and religious convictions, given that there is no book that is
to us quite what Homer was to the Greeks, given that his

account of proportion or harmony is largely formal and in-
sufficiently expounded, so that in the case of the plastic
arts and pure music at least it is impossible to state
with any pretentions to accuracy what examples he would
have approved or disapproved - given all this, it would be
unrealistic to claim that we can say what Plato today
would have felt about specific works of art. But we can,
I think, risk some general observations and suggestions.

It is, for instance, a reasonable inference that an
artistic creed such as the following would have been re-
pugnant to Plato. Malcolm Cowley offers the following
summary of propositions which represent the aesthetic
attitude of the Harvard Aesthetes: 'The cultivation and
expression of his own sensibility are the only justifiable
aims for a poet. Originality is his principle virtue.
Society is stupid, hostile and unmanageable... from which
it is the poet's duty to remain aloof. The poet should
deliberately make himself misunderstandable' (quoted in
Williams, 1971). As against this sort of creed, which
incidentally Plato would probably have interpreted as a
symptom of alienation and anomie in society, Plato is
laying an obligation and a responsibility on the artist
to inspire towards an ideal; artistic skill is not, for
him, enough.

It is also, I think, a reasonable inference that Plato
would at least question the widespread study of literature, in the sense of items from a corpus of generally
accredited 'good books', in our schools. Why do we demand
such study? Of course many answers, which unfortunately
cannot be reviewed here, might be given. But Plato's
argument would seem likely to lead him to reject any claim
that involved either the suggestion that literature might
be an important vehicle for moral education or the suggestion that it might contribute to increasing our
knowledge. In so far as literature presents us with
characters facing moral dilemmas, or with insights into
people's motivation and behaviour, which, of course, it
frequently does, it puts forward moral viewpoints (however
tentative, or even negative) and claims about what people
are, or at least may be, like. Plato's argument seems to
demand the rejoinder that familiarity with moral viewpoints does not constitute understanding the sphere of
morality, quite apart from his fundamental claim that an
author cannot be in a position to write knowledgeably of
moral matters if he has not studied moral philosophy.
Similarly the author, qua literary artist, does not know
anything about human nature. What he is offering us,
unless he happens also to be a philosopher and a student
of human nature, is merely a picture of how the world
appears to him.

This view may seem fantastic to many readers. And certainly one might make out a case for the study of literature even accepting Plato's basic points. For example, one could argue that in practice any decision as to how to act rightly presupposes such basic information as what is likely to happen if one does this rather than that, or that moral maturity demands sensitivity to others as well as intellectual ability, and that literature might contribute to developing one's awareness of others: to developing the affective side of one's nature rather than the cognitive. But it has seemed to me worth stressing Plato's point that to treat of examples of certain kinds of behaviour in literature is not to examine morality itself, that to do that is a philosophical undertaking, and that if we are going to take the literary artist seriously in relation to such matters, he at least, and preferably we as well, ought to have done our philosophical homework.

At the other extreme one feels fairly confident that Plato would have scorned much so-called creative activity in schools in the sphere of arts. In the first place, of course, he would join the swelling band of those who want to know precisely what is meant by this vague term (Barrow, 1975). But assuming it to mean something like self-expression, as it appears to to those who say that 'We cannot deny the epithet "creative" to the five year old child's picture of square cows and neckless mums and dads' (Lytton, 1971, p.3), he would argue that there is nothing necessarily intrinsically valuable about self-expression in whatever medium, but rather that what matters is to tutor the individual so that his 'expression' does become valuable by virtue of the fact that it measures up to standards of competence and, where appropriate, truth and moral rectitude. Furthermore, given his general attitude to the arts it is probable that Plato would have questioned any underlying assumption that what the world needs now is creative artists. Such an attitude would not, of course, be incompatible with the view that creative activity, in the sense in question, has a place in education on therapeutic or psychological grounds (see White, 1972).

The above remarks represent only tentative suggestions, but it seemed worth stressing the probable degree of divergence between Plato and much current thinking related to the sphere of art and art education. I have tried to suggest both in this chapter and in the previous discussion of Plato's theory of knowledge that there is something of importance in his claim that real understanding of such things as courage, religion and morality

in general requires philosophical enquiry. But it is
clear that the crucial question to be asked of Plato is
whether his view of the possibility of moral knowledge,
on which his whole theory is constructed, is or is not
hopelessly astray. How are we supposed to know the moral
truth and hence judge 'right opinion'?

Chapter eight

Moral upbringing

CAN VIRTUE BE TAUGHT?

'Can virtue be taught?' This is a question that re-
appears, explicitly or implicitly in many of the early
dialogues. Both Gorgias and Protagoras, for instance,
in the dialogues bearing their names, claim to be able
to teach virtue. The question is central to the 'Meno'
which opens abruptly with these words: 'Can you tell me,
Socrates, whether virtue can be taught? or is it something acquired by practice? or is it something that can't
by acquired by teaching or practice, but just a natural
aptitude or something else?'

But Socrates does not have an easy answer. On the one
hand if virtue is something that can be taught then there
must be somebody who can teach it. But who are the
teachers of virtue? The suggestion that those who are
wise and good themselves can teach others to be virtuous
seems to be contradicted by the fact that so many good
men have failed to bring up their own children to be
virtuous. 'Take Pericles - a great and wise man. He had
two sons whom he taught riding, music and athletics and
other such things to the point at which they were as
skilled as anybody else in Athens. Didn't he want to
make them good men too? Without doubt he would have
liked to' ('Meno', 94.B). But he did not succeed. 'I
could cite many others too, excellent men themselves, who
none the less failed to make any of their family or anyone
else for that matter, any better' ('Protagoras', 320.B).

Are the sophists, then, such as Protagoras and Gorgias,
able to teach virtue, as they claim? Here too Socrates'
answer is no. If somebody is able to teach something then
he must have knowledge or understanding of that something.
The mere ability to do something oneself does not enable
one to teach others how to do it. Even with a simple

skill such as horse-riding, in order to be able to pass
this on to others it will be necessary to articulate what
has to be done when and why. One's own natural ability,
if one has it, cannot be communicated. But the sophists,
according to Socrates, do not have the necessary understanding and knowledge of virtue. Many of them are mere
charlatans, but even the best of them do not seem to be
able to give an account of what virtue is; they do not
even appear to have a very clear idea of what constitutes
knowledge. How can they teach something that they do not
properly understand themselves? No, for the most part at
least, the sophists are teaching something quite different - the art of persuasive oratory, perhaps - but
certainly not virtue.

So, since nobody appears to be in a position to teach
virtue, the conclusion appears to be that it cannot be
taught. On the other hand Plato and almost certainly the
historical Socrates are firmly wedded to the notion that
virtue is knowledge and therefore can be taught. And
furthermore, says Socrates, in the 'Protagoras', though
the claim is reiterated throughout Plato's dialogues, 'I
am confident that no wise man could believe that anyone
willingly does wrong or performs any evil or unjust
action' ('Protagoras', 345.E).

Faced with the two apparently contradictory propositions that virtue is knowledge and can be taught but
that there are no teachers and therefore it cannot be
taught, Socrates concludes the discussion in the 'Meno'
by suggesting that for some purposes correct opinion may
serve as well as knowledge. He explains this point as
follows: 'If someone knows the way to a particular
place such as Larissa then evidently his knowledge will
enable him to act as a reliable guide to others. But
surely if a man were to opine correctly which road to
take, even though he does not in fact know that it is,
he would also prove a capable guide' ('Meno, 97.B). So,
although correct opinion or true belief must not be con-
fused with knowledge, it can be as good a guide as
knowledge for the purpose of acting rightly. Socrates
therefore puts forward the hypothesis that those good
and wise men to whom they have referred in the discussion
acquired their virtue through true belief. They did not
have knowledge, which explains why they could not pass on
their goodness. 'Their position in relation to knowledge
is no different from that of prophet and tellers of
oracles, who under divine inspiration utter many truths,
but have no knowledge of what they are saying' ('Meno',
99.C). But this hypothesis leaves open the possibility
that there could be teachers of virtue, even though none

are to be found at present. For where there is the possibility of true belief there is in principle the possibility of knowledge. The conclusion for the present is that
'virtue is neither acquired by nature nor teaching. Those
who are virtuous are so by some kind of divine dispen-
sation.' If there were to be a statesman who could teach
others his own virtue he would be, like Tiresias among the
dead, 'a solid reality among shadows' ('Meno', 100.A).

AN ABSOLUTIST ETHICAL THEORY

The two maxims 'virtue is knowledge' and 'no one willingly does wrong' encapsulate the theory that stands opposed
to the relativist ethical theories canvassed by many of
the sophists. Socrates would not accept that morality
was a matter of arbitrary choice by societies or individuals. The claim that virtue is knowledge implies both that
it is in principle possible to know what is good and a
fortiori that there is some absolute moral good. Conjoin-
ed with the other maxim the theory involves the claim that
there is ultimately no such thing as the possibility of
moral conflict, but rather that there are certain moral
principles that cohere with each other and such that,
could we but arrive at knowledge of them, would guarantee
our virtuous behaviour. To recognise the good would be
to do it.
      In the 'Republic', as we have seen, Plato effectively
restates this theory in uncompromising tone. The philosopher-kings are the equivalent of Tiresias in the land of
the living. They are in a position to teach virtue (or
to see that it can be taught) for their goodness is not
based simply on right opinion. They know the good; they
understand the nature of the virtue they exhibit, for
they have been trained in dialectic and thereby come to
know the form of Good (the essential nature of goodness).
That is why they superintend the laws of the state and it
is why they are empowered to take such positive steps with
the children of the state in respect of their moral upbringing.
      Unfortunately the theory contains certain problems.
One was noted by Aristotle and that is that it is
questionable whether, even if it were true that virtue was
knowledge, it would follow that people only do wrong as a
result of ignorance. It is true that part of what we
indicate when we describe an action as good is that we
recognise an obligation to perform such an act rather
than its opposite. It would be logically odd to assert
that a certain action was right and yet to claim that one

could see no reason for doing it. But there is also such
a thing as weakness of will, such that a man may know
what he ought to do, but consciously fail to do it.
Surely this would be an example of willingly doing wrong?

But a much more fundamental problem arises over the
claim that virtue is knowledge itself, for as we saw in
chapter 6, there are good grounds for claiming, as against
Plato, that it is not possible to talk of knowing the
good.

THE STATUS OF MORAL PROPOSITIONS

Since the time of Plato philosophers have, as it were,
pursued the path of dialectic in the hope that they would
arrive at the vision of the Good promised by Plato. Some
have thought that they have attained to it, which is to
say that they have thought that they have hit upon the
fundamental and unchanging principles of morality. What
they have invariably failed to do is convince everybody
else of the correctness of their vision. What they have
been unable to do is to establish beyond reasonable doubt
that they are right. Conceivably some one of them has
had true belief, but none of them could confidently claim
to have had knowledge, for they could not produce incontestable evidence.

In this century most philosophers have accepted the
conclusion that such knowledge cannot be attained. Some,
such as the intuitionists, preserve the basic Platonic
claim that there are absolute moral truths, but argue
that these can only be intuited (or 'known', in an ex-
tended sense, by intuition). Others have concentrated on
suggesting that certain formal principles at least are
presupposed by moral language; on this view, although we
cannot know or establish that people ought to do this or
that specifically, we can establish procedural rules such
as that people ought to be impartial. Others again have
taken the view that there are no absolute truths to be
found, but rather that values are the product of a culture
without any absolute or eternal validity. An extreme
variant of this last view has been proposed according to
which a judgment such as 'freedom is good' is not true or
false, and logically cannot be so, in any way. Thus Ayer
writes, 'It is impossible to find a criterion for determining the validity of ethical judgments...not because they
have an "absolute" validity which is mysteriously inde-
pendent of ordinary sense experience, but because they
have no objective validity whatsoever. If a sentence
makes no statement at all, there is obviously no sense in
asking whether what it says is true or false' (Ayer, 1936,
p.144).

With the plausibility or otherwise of these views, all
of which, incidentally, seem to have been recognised by
Plato as possible points of view, we are not here concerned. What is common to all of them is the basic premise
that moral propositions are a prime example of unprovable
propositions. Whether with the intuitionists we say that
they may be true, but their truth has to be sensed by the
mind, or, with the emotivists, that they are literary non-
sense judged as statements, we agree that we do not know
what would count as conclusive evidence. That the battle
of Hastings was fought in 1066 may be disputed, but there
would be no dispute about the kind of evidence that would
be relevant for or against such a claim. The same cannot
be said of a claim such as that freedom is good.

It is very important to stress that this admission
does not lead to the conclusion that the moral relativists
are correct. By the same token that we cannot prove con-
clusively that X is good, we cannot prove that X is not
good in some absolute sense. Just as we cannot prove that
the intuitionists are correct, so we cannot prove that
relativists or emotivists are. These are theories which
in the nature of things we can do no more than examine
minutely for their plausibility, and it is still, therefore, an open question as to whether there are or are not
some things that people just ought to do or refrain from
doing, or whether it makes sense to claim that there are.
Consequently the objection to Plato is not necessarily
that he wrongly believed in absolute moral principles,
nor indeed that his actual values were therefore necessarily merely his arbitrary preferences. Rather the
objection is to his assumption that the philosopher-kings
will as a matter of fact be able to know what is good -
the assumption that there can be experts in morals who
know what is morally good as there are experts in medicine
who know what is medically sound.

MORAL UPBRINGING IN THE 'REPUBLIC'

In the light of this objection what are we to make of the
moral upbringing advocated in the 'Republic'? For it
seems that we are being asked to accept that what is good
shall be determined by people who logically cannot in
fact know what is good.

In what does the moral upbringing of a child in the
Republic consist? First, he is a member of a society in
which there is no plurality of values or divergence of
moral opinion such as we are accustomed to. The values
and rules of the society are uniformly accepted and acted

upon, with the result that the child is subject to a consistent example as an influence. Second, the stories that
he is told have been carefully censored to reinforce that
influence, and all works of art with which he comes into
contact are similarly selected with reference to their
propensity to influence him towards the good. Third, he
is told the 'noble lie' (414), according to which all
children were born of mother earth, but they were born
with different metals in their souls: gold in the soul
betokening the nature of a ruler, silver the nature of an
auxiliary, copper and bronze the nature suitable to
membership of the largest group of producers. The significance of this myth is clearly intended to convey the
message that on the one hand people are different and
their differences may constitute relevant reasons for
their performing different functions in life, but on the
other hand that they are none the less all brothers, all
equally important in their own way. The function of the
myth is evidently also to instil the conviction that all
is for the best in the best of all possible worlds.
    For the majority, and that includes the auxiliaries at
this point, this programme of moral upbringing, remarkable
in its similarity to the contemporary Russian system, is
all that they ever receive. They are inculcated with what
Plato is pleased to call 'right opinion', in accordance
with his conviction that there is an absolute moral truth
that can be known. The select few come, at a later stage,
to examine the matter for themselves and to see that the
'right opinion' that has been cultivated in them is indeed
right, again in accordance with Plato's view of the nature
of morality.

PRELIMINARY POINTS

There are two preliminary points that need to be made
before we attempt to assess this programme. First, it is
the principles only that here concern me. I do not intend
to discuss the merits or demerits of Plato's actual moral
values (i.e. the substance of 'right opinion'), except in
so far as they are necessarily enshrined in his procedure.
Nor do I intend to take seriously the suggestion that we
make use of Homer, and tell our children Plato's noble
lie. The interesting question is whether in principle
this kind of procedure is morally acceptable or not.
    Second, I do not intend to pursue the empirical
question of whether this procedure would work, in the
sense of succeed in implanting fixed adherences to what
the authorities regard as right opinion. Plato's view

that people's attitudes and values are significantly
affected by their surroundings and in particular his view
that people become like the characters in the books or
the plays they admire might be challenged. As it has been
indeed from the time that Aristotle put forward his rival
cathartic theory according to which people purge their un-
savoury emotions - let off steam, as it were, vicarious-
ly - in the theatre. In what follows I work on the hypothesis, which I confess seems to me eminently plausible,
that Plato is substantially correct on this issue, if a
trifle uncompromising in his statement of it. Similarly
the metaphysical speculations of some educationalists that
people are born good is hereby rejected.

My basic premise is that people may grow up to be good
or evil and which they do will depend to some considerable
extent on the nature of the environment, in its widest
sense, in which they grow.

On this assumption what are we to say about censorship?
Without argument, let us agree that we are not in favour
of wholesale censorship by the state and even that we do
not want massive bowdlerising of children's books. Rather
let us ask whether we regard some control over the sort of
material children read as acceptable. Of course in re-
phrasing the question in this way I am considerably modi-
fying the extreme nature of Plato's actual proposals, but
it is only with the principle of such control that we are
here concerned. The sort of question we have to ask ourselves is 'is it conceivable in our view that some books
might seem to be such that we would feel justified in
keeping them out of the way of children?' My suggestion
is that to most of us the answer is 'yes, it is conceivable.' And if that is so, we have thereby accepted
that in principle censorship of children's literature
may be justified, and the only remaining question is the
quite distinct one of to what extent and on precisely
what grounds would it be legitimate to censor.

But I do not in any case feel that the issue of
censorship considered in isolation is crucial here.
Surely the crucial issue is the whole process, for prima
facie what Plato is doing by means of censorship, demanding certain types of behaviour, and telling the noble lie,
is indoctrinating and conditioning the children of the
Republic? And is not that in principle objectionable?

INDOCTRINATION

I doubt whether Plato can have intended the theory of
forms to apply to all concepts. Certainly it is difficult
to see how it could apply to a complex abstraction such as

'indoctrination'. Be that as it may, philosophers
certainly have not found the form of indoctrination if
there is one. On the contrary, between them they have
produced a wide variety of conceptions or criteria for the
use of the term. Broadly speaking, all are agreed on the
basic point that to indoctrinate involves implanting
beliefs. Thereafter some claim that only certain kinds
of beliefs can be indoctrinated, namely belief in unprovable propositions or more specifically doctrinal
beliefs; some claim that indoctrination can only take
place if non-rational means of persuasion are used; some
claim that the hallmark of indoctrination lies in the aim
to evoke unshakeable commitment to a belief. And others
offer various combinations of these three proposed
criteria.

On almost any view, however, the philosopher-kings in
the Republic are being indoctrinated, and on literally any
view the mass of the people are. For they are being
imbued with beliefs that, being moral, are unprovable, by
methods which clearly do not (indeed cannot) involve
rational demonstration of their truth, and the intention
is that these beliefs shall be indelibly imprinted on
their consciousness like a dye. The philosopher-kings
alone could be said not to be indoctrinated, if we were
to accept the intentional analysis of the concept, which
says that to indoctrinate one must intend to close the
mind of the person being indoctrinated in such a way that
they will never come to the point of genuinely examining
the matter rationally for themselves. For, of course, in
theory, the philosopher-kings do ultimately, and are
intended to, do this.

Since on any account, at least some of Plato's citizens
are being indoctrinated, the next question and the only
important question is whether that is objectionable. Some
might claim that indoctrination is objectionable by definition. But this, I think, will not do. Since it does
not obviously even mean one thing and one thing only, it
is difficult to accept that any view of what indoctrination is must necessarily be morally objectionable. The
more so as some people, at various times, quite clearly
have not used the word pejoratively. The pejorative over-
tones that it probably does have for most people in our
society at this time are surely a contingent factor. We
happen to disapprove of what we vaguely regard as indoctrination. But the question that needs answering is
whether we have good reason to take moral objection to
what Plato in principle proposes, whether we call it indoctrination or anything else. And my answer to that
question is a rather unfashionable 'No.'

My reasoning is as follows: let us take a proposition such as 'killing is wrong' as an example of the sort of proposition that Plato would have us bring up children to believe to be true. We have accepted as a premise that we are not in a position to claim that it is known to be true; likewise that it is not known whether an absolutist view, such as intuitionism, or a relativist view is correct. That being the case it is necessary to defend Plato's procedure with reference to both viewpoints.

If we take the relativist view then we have to work on the assumption that the proposition 'killing is wrong' does not represent some objective truth about killing that is true for all people at all times whether they realise it or not, but rather represents a disapproving attitude to killing that a particular society happens to have. Those who object to Plato's procedure would presumably argue that since the view that killing is wrong is just a convention or a norm that society adopts, because it happens to have a distaste for such activity, it is objectionable to treat it as some kind of truth. But, if the relativists are correct, then it is true that 'killing people is wrong' in our society, because our society has this norm. And, if it is just a matter of taste, there seems no more reason to object to imparting this moral taste to our children than to object to imparting our culinary, musical or sporting tastes. It surely cannot be wrong to cultivate a taste for, say, Beethoven. Besides which, on the relativist view, to say that it would be wrong to impart musical or moral taste would be demonstrably false, for on this view 'wrong' means 'disapproved of by society' - and it simply is not true that society in general disapproves of such cultivation of moral attitudes. To say that society ought to disapprove is at once to move away from the relativist position into some branch of the absolutist camp.

If we adopt an absolutist view, such that we claim that the proposition is just true, but we acknowledge that it cannot be proved or strictly speaking known to be true, the situation is different. On this view it may be argued that, since we believe that moral propositions have objective validity but do not think the truth of any particular proposition can be unequivocally proved true, we ought to allow individuals to form their own opinions. This argument I shall assume to be valid up to a point. But to talk of forming opinions in any meaningful sense in matters where it is presumed, as here, that the matter is not purely arbitrary, involves competence within the sphere. One cannot sensibly talk of a person who knows nothing about art and nothing about aesthetics forming

his own opinion on what paintings are beautiful, even if
we concede that the aesthetic sphere is essentially subjective. Still less can we reasonably claim that, on the
one hand, the moral sphere is more than a collection of
conventional fiats, and that, on the other hand, children
who know little about the historical facts relating to
moral systems and nothing relating to the philosophical
competence necessary to examining the validity and status
of ethical claims should make up their own mind on the
matter. They are not in a position to make informed
judgments or to have informed opinions on the matter.

The truth is that, whichever way one looks at it, the
question of what is the moral truth, which encompasses
the question of whether there is such a thing as moral
truth, is a highly sophisticated philosophical question.
And Plato is quite right to say that it cannot profitably
be examined by children. Such enquiry belongs to a later
stage of education. In which case what are we to do with
young children? Whatever we might fancy we would like to
do, we presumably have to face the fact that children
will develop moral attitudes and beliefs. That is to say
they will develop attitudes of approval, disapproval or
indifference to the ways of behaving that come into the
category of moral behaviour. That being the case the
only question of principle that there is to be answered
is 'should we cultivate approval of what we approve or
not?' It is difficult to find a convincing reason for
saying that we should not.

Where there does seem good reason to depart from Plato,
however, is over his view that for most people the matter
can be left there. For given that it seems clear that
Plato's view that incontestable moral knowledge is
possible is unacceptable, then the very premium on pursuing rational understanding and knowledge that he places
demands that in a sphere that is so complex and so uncertain people should be initiated into it. The vision
of the Good may perhaps not be vouchsafed to us, but it
is our bounden duty to search for it.

SUMMARY

In the view of virtually all contemporary philosophers
Plato is mistaken in his claim that the Good can be
'known', if we take knowledge to be true belief backed by
adequate evidence, since there is too little agreement
about what kind of evidence is even relevant, let alone
adequate, to establishing the truth of moral propositions.
He may, of course, also be wrong in assuming that there

are any moral principles of eternal and absolute validity;
but on this point philosophers are divided and we cannot
legitimately assume that he is certainly wrong. The
question is, therefore, whether the admission that moral
knowledge is not so far as we can see attainable destroys
the educational edifice that Plato has painstakingly constructed: does it mean that the consummation of the educational programme (the pursuit of the idea of the Good)
is an empty exercise? that nobody can be in a position
to determine the justice or injustice of the educational
arrangements in the Republic? that the programme of moral
education amounts to the blind dictating to the blind?
and that the attempt to inculcate 'right opinion' through
the arts amounts to an arbitrary decision to inculcate
the opinion of the powers that be?

I shall conclude by offering the suggestion that although Plato may have been mistaken about the possibility
of moral knowledge, his educational programme is not necessarily thereby invalidated. For although nobody may
be in a position to lay claim to knowledge of what is
morally good, we may surely distinguish between those who
have expertise in examining such questions and those who
do not. There is still a distinction to be drawn between
informed and ill-informed opinion in this sphere as in
others; there is still a distinction to be made between
reasonable and unreasonable arguments. If such a line of
thought were to be accepted then, it seems to me, the
substance and the principles of Plato's educational view,
if not the details, represent a formidable argument that
cannot be lightly ignored or dismissed.

Suggestions for further reading

General books on Plato's philosophy are legion.
A.E.Taylor, 'Plato: The Man and His Work' (Methuen,
1926), still provides one of the best comprehensive intro-
ductions to the dialogues. I.M.Crombie, 'An Examination
of Plato's Doctrines' (Routledge & Kegan Paul, 1962), is
to be particularly recommended for a detailed and impartial exposition of key aspects of Plato's thought.
Also useful are G.C.Field, 'The Philosophy of Plato'
(Oxford, 1969) and G.M.A.Grube, 'Plato's Thought'
(Methuen, 1970). R.Cross and A.D.Woozley, 'Plato's Republic: A Philosophical Commentary' (Macmillan, 1964) is
a useful introductory guide to the philosophy of that dialogue.
   There have also been many contributions to the question
of the nature of the philosophy of education, touched upon
in the introductory chapter. C.J.Lucas (ed.), 'What is
Philosophy of Education?' (Collier-Macmillan, 1969) con-
tains a valuable collection of papers. See also
R.G.Woods, Philosophy of Education in R.G.Woods (ed.),
'Education and its Disciplines' (University of London
Press, 1972), K.Thompson, Philosophy of Education and Edu-
cational Practice in the 'Proceedings of the Philosophy of
Education Society of Great Britain' ('PESGB'), 1970,
vol.4, and R.Barrow, What's Wrong with the Philosophy of
Education? in the 'British Journal of Educational
Studies', vol.22, June 1974.
   For the historical background to Plato's formative
years, see either W.G.Forrest, 'The Emergence of Greek
Democracy' (Weidenfeld & Nicolson, 1966) or R.Barrow,
'Athenian Democracy' (Macmillan, 1973). An altogether
more detailed account of the sophists is provided by
W.K.C.Guthrie, 'The Sophists' (Cambridge, 1971). Also
worth reading are the opening chapters of R.H.S.Crossman,
'Plato Today' (Allen & Unwin, 1963).

Crossman's 'Plato Today' is essentially concerned with criticism of the 'Republic'. It is one of a number of books which, despite their undeniable importance, need watching, since they run neutral exposition and personal interpretation of the 'Republic' alarmingly close together. K.R.Popper, 'The Open Society and its Enemies', vol.1 (Routledge & Kegan Paul, 1966) is perhaps the most notable example of a vigorous but at times idiosyncratic interpretation. See also, as a counterweight to Popper and Crossman, R.Barrow, 'Plato, Utilitarianism and Education' (Routledge & Kegan Paul, 1975). I.M.Crombie's summary of the 'Republic' in 'An Examination of Plato's Doctrines', vol.1, is judicious.

For discussion of the concepts of equality and impartiality, central to chapter 4, see: S.I.Benn and R.S.Peters, 'Social Principles and the Democratic State' (Allen & Unwin, 1959), ch.5; R.S.Peters, 'Ethics and Education' (Allen & Unwin, 1966), ch.4; and J.Gribble, 'Introduction to the Philosophy of Education' (Allyn & Bacon, 1969). See also R.Barrow, 'Moral Philosophy for Education' (Allen & Unwin, 1975), chs 5 and 13 for a more specific treatment of the question of equality in education. R.S.Peters, 'Ethics and Education', pt 1 is also the locus classicus for Peters' views on the concept of education, notwithstanding the fact that he has modified his position in more recent writings. Woods and Dray offer some trenchant criticism of Peters' approach in R.S.Peters (ed.), 'The Philosophy of Education' (Oxford, 1973). See also R.G.Woods and R.Barrow, 'An Introduction to Philosophy of Education' (Methuen, 1975), ch.1. A moderate course is steered by W.K.Frankena, The Concept of Education Today in J.F.Doyle (ed.), 'Educational Judgments' (Routledge & Kegan Paul, 1973). J.P.White, Intelligence and the Logic of the Nature-Nurture Issue in 'PESGB', vol.8, no.1, January 1974 is an interesting contemporary view of this matter. For further discussion of the role of nature/nurture in Plato's educational theory, see H.D.Rankin, 'Plato and the Individual' (Methuen, 1964). K.R.Popper, 'The Open Society', argues strenuously for the view that the Republic is an objectionable kind of class society, while R.Barrow, 'Plato, Utilitarianism and Education', seeks to rebut the charge. Also pertinent to this topic is the discussion of the concept of an elite in R.G.Woods and R.Barrow, 'An Introduction to the Philosophy of Education', ch.9.

Many of the concepts considered in chapter 5 relating to teaching methodology are admirably examined by R.F.Dearden, 'The Philosophy of Primary Education' (Routledge & Kegan Paul, 1968). See also his paper on

Instruction and Learning by Discovery in R.S.Peters (ed.),
'The Concept of Education' (Routledge & Kegan Paul, 1972)
and his paper The Concept of Play in the same volume.
Note also N.Gayer and M.F.Burnyeat, Play and Pleasure,
'PESGB', vol.5, no.1, 1971. Discussions of the broader
issue of freedom in education that lies behind much of the
content of this chapter are to be found in: R.S.Peters,
'Ethics and Education', ch.7; R.Barrow, 'Moral Philosophy
for Education', chs 4 and 12; and J.Gribble, 'Introduction to Philosophy of Education', ch.6b.
    A short but excellent comment on Plato's concept of
dialectic is to be found in I.M.Crombie, 'An Examination
of Plato's Doctrines', vol.1, pp.129-31. Indispensable
for a serious study of this matter is R.Robinson, 'Plato's
Earlier Dialectic' (Oxford, 1953). Relevant to this topic
as it is discussed in the text are: N.Postman and
C.Weingartner, 'Teaching as a Subversive Activity'
(Penguin, 1971) and R.G.Woods and R.Barrow, 'An Introduction to the Philosophy of Education', ch.5, on ration-
ality.
    A sober treatment of the concepts of truth and
knowledge is provided by J.Hospers, 'An Introduction to
Philosophical Analysis' (Routledge & Kegan Paul, 1956),
ch.2. Plato's theory of ideas is discussed in G.C.Field,
'The Philosophy of Plato', chs 1 and 2, and in
I.M.Crombie, 'An Examination of Plato's Doctrines', vol.1,
(see index, under Forms). A more comprehensive and detailed analysis is provided by W.D.Ross, 'Plato's Theory
of Ideas'(Oxford, 1951). P.H.Hirst's Liberal Education
and the Nature of Knowledge' has been most recently re-
printed in P.H.Hirst, 'Knowledge and the Curriculum'
(Routledge & Kegan Paul, 1975). For criticism of Hirst,
see J.P.White, 'Towards a Compulsory Curriculum' (Routledge & Kegan Paul, 1973), ch.6 and further references
cited in the suggestions for further reading in that
volume.
    J.Hospers, 'Meaning and Truth in the Arts' (Chapel
Hill, 1946) and V.C.Aldrich, 'Philosophy of Art' (Pren-
tice-Hall, 1963) provide good discussions of the main
philosophical problems in this area. For a further discussion of Plato's theory of art, see G.M.A.Grube,
'Plato's Thought', ch.6. On creativity see R.Barrow,
'Moral Philosophy for Education', ch.10. The wider rami-
fications of aesthetics and education are pursued in:
'Philosophy and the Teaching of the Arts', report of a
conference, published by ATCDE; S.Gregor, Aesthetic
Meaning in 'PESGB', vol.6, no.2; and L.Arnaud Reid,
Knowledge, Aesthetic Insight and Education in 'PESGB',
vol.7, no.1.

On the underlying problem of the status of moral
judgments, see R.Barrow, 'Moral Philosophy for Education',
chs 2 and 3. For discursive accounts of ethical theories,
see R.S.Peters, 'Ethics and Education', ch.3, and
G.Warnock, 'Contemporary Moral Philosophy' (Macmillan,
1967). For Plato's ethical theory, see G.C.Field, 'The
Philosophy of Plato', chs 1-5. I.A.Snook (ed.), 'Concepts
of Indoctrination' (Routledge & Kegan Paul, 1972) is an
invaluable collection of contemporary papers on indoctrination. R.Barrow, 'Plato, Utilitarianism and Education',
esp.ch.6, attempts a full-scale defence of Plato's use of
indoctrination. For a variety of approaches to moral education, see: G.Ryle, Can Virtue be Taught? in R.F.Dear-
den, P.H.Hirst and R.S.Peters (eds), Education and the
Development of Reason' (Routledge & Kegan Paul, 1972);
R.Barrow, 'Moral Philosophy for Education', ch.14;
R.F.Dearden, 'The Philosophy of Primary Education', ch.8;
and J.Gribble, 'Introduction to Philosophy of Education',
ch.5.

Penguin Books publish a number of Plato's dialogues in
translation. Those with a feeling for style, however,
may well prefer Jowett's famous translations, some of
which are available in four volumes from Sphere paper-
backs.

Bibliography

AYER, A.J. (1936), 'Language, Truth and Logic', Victor
Gollancz.
BARROW, R. (1973), 'Athenian Democracy', Macmillan.
BARROW, R. (1974), Who are the Philosopher-Kings?, 'Pro-
ceedings of the Philosophy of Education Society of Great
Britian', vol.8, no.2, July.
BARROW, R. (1975), 'Moral Philosophy for Education',
Allen & Unwin.
BOSANQUET, B. (1900), 'The Education of the Young in
Plato's Republic', Cambridge.
CROMBIE, I.M. (1962), 'An Examination of Plato's
Doctrines', 2 vols, Routledge & Kegan Paul.
DEARDEN, R.F. (1967), Instruction and Learning by Dis-
covery in R.S.Peters (ed.), 'The Concept of Education',
Routledge & Kegan Paul.
HARE, R.M. (1970), 'The Dialogues of Plato', introduction,
Sphere Books.
HIRST, P.H. (1972), Liberal Education and the Nature of
Knowledge in R.F.Dearden, P.H.Hirst and R.S.Peters (eds),
'Education and the Development of Reason', Routledge &
Kegan Paul.
HIRST, P.H. (1973), What is Teaching? in R.S.Peters (ed.),
'The Philosophy of Education', Oxford.
LYTTON, H. (1971), 'Creativity and Education', Routledge &
Kegan Paul.
PETERS, R.S. (1966), 'Ethics and Education', Allen &
Unwin.
POPPER, K.R. (1966),'The Open Society and Its Enemies',
2 vols, Routledge & Kegan Paul.
POSTMAN, N. and WEINGARTNER, C. (1971), 'Teaching as a
Subversive Activity', Penguin Books.
RANKIN, H.D. (1969), 'Plato and the Individual', Methuen.
RUSSELL, B. (1946), 'A History of Western Philosophy',
Allen & Unwin.

SHOREY, P. (1935), 'Plato's Republic', introduction and
translation, 2 vols, Heinemann.
SHOREY, P. (1965), 'What Plato Said' (abridged edition),
University of Chicago Press.
WHITE, J.P. (1972), Creativity and Education in R.F.Dear-
den, P.H.Hirst and R.S.Peters (eds), 'Education and the
Development of Reason', Routledge & Kegan Paul.
WILLIAMS, D. (1971), 'Trousered Apes', Churchill Press.